i♥geeks

i ♥ geeks

THE OFFICIAL HANDBOOK

CARRIE TUCKER

Adamsmedia
Avon, Massachusetts

Published by
Adams Media, an F+W Media Company
57 Littlefield Street, Avon, MA 02322. U.S.A.
www.adamsmedia.com

ISBN-10: 1-60550-023-2
ISBN-13: 978-1-60550-023-2

Printed in the United States of America.

J I H G F E D C B A

Library of Congress Cataloging-in-Publication Data
is available from the publisher.

This publication is designed to provide accurate and authoritative information with regard to the subject matter covered. It is sold with the understanding that the publisher is not engaged in rendering legal, accounting, or
other professional advice. If legal advice or other expert assistance is required,
the services of a competent professional person should be sought.

—From a *Declaration of Principles* jointly adopted by a Committee of the
American Bar Association and a Committee of Publishers and Associations

Many of the designations used by manufacturers and sellers to distinguish
their product are claimed as trademarks. Where those designations appear in
this book and Adams Media was aware of a trademark claim, the designations
have been printed with initial capital letters.

Interior illustrations by Daniel Tero.

This book is available at quantity discounts for bulk purchases.
For information, please call 1-800-289-0963.

CONTENTS

CHAPTER 1 · 1

"A long time ago in a galaxy far, far away . . ."

The Evolution of Geeks

CHAPTER 2 · 13

"Can I just finish this level?"

Video Game Geeks

ACKNOWLEDGMENTS

I'd like to thank my boyfriend, Steve Hahnel, for inspiration and for allowing me to hog the Netflix; Carrie Borzillo-Vrenna, for getting this whole thing started and without whom this never would have happened; Dr. and Mrs. Tucker for always encouraging me, even when it seemed impractical and logic-defying; and my agent, Holly Root, for believing—without her this really never would have happened.

Thanks to everyone who contributed, helped out, or allowed me to ask numerous annoying questions: Jessicka and Christian Addams, Miguel Banuelos, Rachel Bigler and The Anime Blog, Elisa Collacott and Watching *Doctor Who*, Jonathan Coulton, Keith Cunningham, Stacey Frost and Iz McAuliffe from *Comic Racks*, Ken Hahn, Kevin Jolly, Jennifer Kashdan, Kristin, Julie, Dr. Randall Osborne, Diana Perry, Jason Pettigrew, Joe Price, Raph Soohoo, Kerry Shapleigh, Cailin and Eric Stamile, Sara, Anne Wirtz, and Sunny Zobel.

Extra-special-super-happy thanks to friends who went above and beyond: Jimmy Aquino and *Comic News Insider*, Christina Guerin for patiently reading, Piney Kahn, Cat Kinney, and Brendan Mobert.

I Love Geeks is dedicated to the late Gary Gygax (1938–2008), creator of Dungeons & Dragons, an inspiration to geeks and nerds everywhere.

1. You met your man via:

a. Jdate, of course. Your mother would be so proud!

b. The WoW message board. Not like he had much time to chat.

c. When you had to call geek patrol because your stupid computer crashed or something.

d. Nerdpassions.com You were charmed by his passionate debate on who's the best superhero: Gambit or Supes (um, Superman).

e. A Halloween party. He was the shy wallflower dressed as an elf.

2. It's Sunday, and beautiful outside. The sun is shining, there's a nice breeze. Your man wants to:

a. Take you on a bike ride or spend the day with Bill Simmons

b. Get on Halo immediately to finish what he started the night before

c. Revert the USB kernel extensions on his Mac so he can get his iPod synched up again

d. Watch the entire Spider-Man trilogy for the fifth time

e. Plan his outfit for AnimeCon

3. **Your computer keeps telling you "192.158.1.100 in use by 00:16:6f:3d:e8:f1, DHCP Server 192.168.1.1" and won't let you open Word. You:**
   a. Call the Geek Squad
   b. Try to look it up online, you know the value of Google.
   c. Call your man, who says, "Re-boot."
   d. Call your man, who mutters something about 2001 and HAL.
   e. Call your man, who says, "Look it up online."

4. **His favorite movie is:**
   a. Anything directed by Takashi Miike
   b. *Tron*
   c. *The Eternal Sunshine of the Spotless Mind*
   d. *Batman Begins*
   e. *Akira*

5. **His favorite author is:**
   a. James Joyce
   b. John Carmack
   c. Bjarne Stroustrup
   d. J.R.R. Tolkien
   e. Osamu Tezuka

6. **Your man knows who the following are (select all that apply):**
    a. Tim Tebow
    b. Will Wright
    c. Linus Torvalds
    d. Arthur C. Clarke
    e. Son Goku

7. **How long is he on the computer for, not counting work, each day?**
    a. less than one hour
    b. 5-7 hours
    c. 8 hours or more
    d. 1-2 hours
    e. 3-4 hours

8. **Who does your man think would win in a fight?**
    a. Farmer Ted or Brian Ralph (as in puke) Johnson
    b. Kratos or Ares
    c. C++ or Linux
    d. Mothra or Rodan
    e. Light or L

9. **Has your man ever waited in line longer than an hour for any of the following?**
   a. An iPhone
   b. The brand new Xbox 360
   c. A new hard drive
   d. *Star Wars: The Phantom Menace*
   e. The *X-Files* panel at Comic-Con

10. **Your man has participated in the following sports:**
   a. Baseball
   b. Table Tennis, bowling, golf….all on the Wii
   c. Online chess. What, it's totally a sport!
   d. Squeezing one of those mushy balls when he's stressed
   e. Firing ping-pong balls from his SD Gundam's Vulcan cannon

11. **Can your man read, write, or spell in any non-traditional language? (Klingon, Elvish, l33t, etc.)**
   a. What the hell?
   b. Yes

12. **Dinner time! What usually happens?**
   a. "Already ate a Manwich."
   b. "No time, not hungry, must finish level, grab me a Mountain Dew?"
   c. "I run on my own fuel."
   d. Grunt: "Nachos."
   e. Grunt: "Pizza."

Scoring:

Mostly A's: He's sorta nerdy, maybe an undercover nerd. Probably likes sports a lot and feels it helps "integrate" him into mainstream society more, although he's never picked up a football in his life. You might laugh when you see him bellow, "Run the ball!" because it seems so out of sorts with his un-ironic "My Mom Thinks I'm Cute" t-shirt and glasses.

Mostly B's: His life is ruled by how many video game accomplishments he can rack up on Xbox360, or how many game hours he can log in a week. Regularly conducts marathon gaming sessions that start at 8 P.M. and end at . . . 8 A.M. THE NEXT DAY.

Mostly C's: Your computer will never need repair, thanks to him. As a matter of fact, your computer has already been repaired within an inch of its life. He wears a t-shirt that says, "There's No Place Like 127.0.0.1."

Mostly D's: Ebert and Roper have nothing on this film nerd. Your idea of a "send-up" is his idea of "homage." He actually still owns the *Star Wars* sheets he slept on as a child . . . and still sleeps on them. He claims he was first attracted to you because you reminded him of Arwen.

Mostly E's: He keeps telling you that comics and anime are art forms— and then you catch him checking out the "booth babes" dressed as slutty Sailor Moons at Comic-Con.

Now, keep in mind, this quiz is for **entertainment purposes only** and full of sweeping generalizations—your guy could be a nerd combo, a blend of any and/or all of said sweeping generalizations, in which case you NEED THIS BOOK the most!

INTRODUCTION

If you picked up this book, it's pretty safe to say that you (like me) love geeks and nerds. You could be (like me) slightly geeky yourself. But even if—especially if—you've never picked up a game controller or a comic book, you've come to the right place. *I Love Geeks* is for the ladies who (duh) love geeks and nerds but aren't quite sure how to find common ground with them. It's about how to get along with your geek or nerd and how eventually to dork out with him. This isn't a book about dating per se. And this is not a book about how you're supposed to like the stuff your guy likes so he'll like you more. No, there are enough of those. This is a book about expanding your horizons. You understand the value of geeks and nerds—I don't need to convince you. You know they run the world, they're loyal as hell, and you find their extreme passions fascinating—well, if you could just understand them a little bit better. And you do want to understand them. You just don't know where to start.

When and How It Started for Me

For me, I guess it all started when I was a kid. At an early age, I displayed a real propensity for learning, and I developed the uncool tendency to get good grades and spend all of my waking hours reading. I loved how stories took me somewhere foreign, somewhere I might never get to go otherwise. My fellow uncool students and I discovered a game that let us act out our fantasies of being somewhere else, of being someone else: Dungeons & Dragons. We also discovered a comic book called *ElfQuest*, which I took to school every week for us to act out during lunch.

I fell in love with fantasy, science fiction, and the improbability of it all. I went to see the original *Star Wars* in the theater when it came out, and I pleaded with my parents for *Star Wars* sheets and action figures. After school, I watched reruns of *Star Trek*, *Lost in Space*, and the bizarre Japanese robot show *Space Giants*. My PhD-holding father opened a computer store in the mid-1980s, where I often "worked." Mostly I vacuumed the carpet. When I wasn't doing that, I was learning DOS and playing the computer game *Wishbringer*. Saddled with ugly glasses that I refused to wear once I left Catholic school and wanted desperately to fit in at junior high, I developed a reputation for being "the snobby new girl," since I never waved to anyone in the hallways. Sadly, I just couldn't see them.

So It Became Official: I Possessed the Beginnings of Nerd-dom

Over the years, I clung to my love of 1970s- and 1980s-era comics, fantasy films and TV shows, reading, and getting good grades. However, as I got older, my priorities shifted, and the urgency of keeping up with the latest comic or being the first in line for *The Lord of the Rings* sort of went by the wayside. But my love of geeks and nerds did not. I always was attracted to nerds' intelligence, their unwillingness to conform, and their ability to introduce me to new things. To me, there is nothing hotter than a brilliant guy with a sense of humor. Although I didn't always share nerds' interests, I often found myself reading up on them so that I could have an intelligent conversation about said interests. Also—and I'm sort of ashamed to admit this because it's not like a woman should really change who she is for a guy, and I never did—I felt a teeny, tiny bit cooler for knowing about obscure stuff that was usually spoken of only in the realm of guys.

So How Far Have I Come and Where Am I Now?

My current boyfriend is a gamer. He spends hours on games—or would like to spend hours on them if I weren't bothering him with pesky questions like "Hey, want to go get some dinner?" and "Hey, want to, um, hang out?" I used to get impatient; I'd huff out of the room, hoping that he'd come to his senses. But then I realized that I sucked for doing that. I mean, how many times had I made him watch *America's Next Top Model*, Olympic gymnastics, and dog shows? Or asked him, "Which one looks better, the heel or the flat?" Poor guy. So out of a desire to compromise and bond with my man, I began searching for tips on video games and sports (though entirely un-jockish, he's sports obsessed—as are many nerds, since they love to collect data, and sports is full of that). The more I dug, the more options I was presented with and the more confusing and convoluted it all became—just like in those *Choose Your Own Adventure* novels (required reading for nerds growing up in the 1980s). I didn't have time for this! I wished for just one place to find it all, the CliffsNotes on guy nerd-dom, so to speak. But it didn't seem to exist, so I decided to just write my own.

CHAPTER 1
"A long time ago in a
galaxy far, far away..."

The Evolution of Geeks

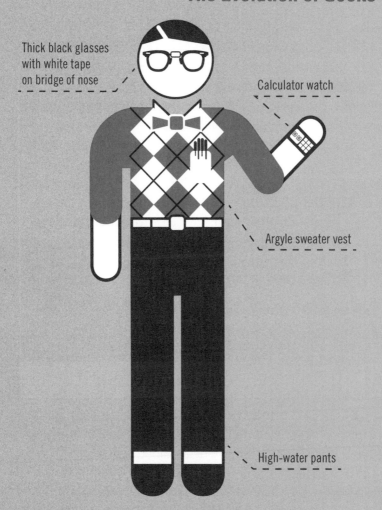

Thick black glasses
with white tape
on bridge of nose

Calculator watch

Argyle sweater vest

High-water pants

Now, before we go any further here, we must distinguish between the words *nerd* and *geek*. Wikipedia defines *nerd* as a "term...that refers to a person who passionately pursues intellectual activities, esoteric knowledge, or other obscure interests that are age inappropriate rather than engaging in more social or popular activities." *Geek* has evolved over time and used to be interchangeable with "nerd." With the rise of technology, the "geek" came to be known as, well, your company's IT guy (or someone supremely mastered in all forms of technology). This love of technology is usually accompanied by stereotypically nerdy interests (more like obsessions) such as playing video games, collecting toys, reading graphic novels, and watching film trilogies.

Nerd or Geek? What's the Difference?

Since a lot of geeks and nerds are sensitive about the designations and in the interest of our little CliffsNotes-style guide you're reading, the terms are used somewhat interchangeably in this book, even though I attempt to apply them correctly whenever possible. Yes, yes, I know that some people think nerds are more intellectual whereas geeks sometimes focus on a single obsession and study it to death. Ladies, I know you don't care either way, but it is pretty important to your guy. Ask him which one he prefers. Some people still might be offended—they feel as though the words are still derogatory and pigeonhole them into a lame stereotype. I'm not saying this is merely a lifestyle; for many of these geeks and nerds, it's their life. But some people claim the labels loud and proud, and don't care who calls them what or who sees them profess enthusiasm for *Firefly*. Those are the types of geeks we love. Enthusiasm is seriously hot.

Nature vs. Nurture: The Evolution of a Culture

So how did geeks and nerds evolve anyway? Is it the old nature vs. nurture argument? It's awfully simplistic to say that society has always put a higher premium on looks than on intelligence. Social skills also are highly valued, so even if your average geek was an attractive individual, if he or she was shy, personal interactions could be downright painful.

"American culture, in particular, stresses looks and athleticism. Any of us who have neither according to the standard are likely to develop introversion, shyness, and even low self-esteem," says Dr. Randall Osborne, a psychology professor at Texas State University-San Marcos. Dr. Osborne has studied the development of the nerd personality and wrote a book called *A Word from the Nerd*. He admits to "living and surviving as a nerd" all his life.

"This introversion, coupled with intelligence and a desire to achieve, however, pushes the nerd to excel in other ways," he says. So it's natural that this kind of person would invest more time in activities that either don't require social interaction (reading, writing, arithmetic) or that bring him or her together with others who share the same traits (science labs, computer clubs). The majority (or non-nerds), uncomfortable with what they can't relate to, relegate these people to the outskirts of their social groups.

So it's both nature *and* nurture? Dr. Osborne offers a simple explanation: "The nature part is the intelligence and the quest to achieve. The nurture part is the push for a certain 'buff' look and athletic prowess. When these collide, we can create a nerd. Intelligence, per se, does not a nerd make, but it is a precondition. Through being ostracized, rejected, teased incessantly, etc., one retreats further inward. Social skills are minimal at best. Efforts to fit in are often disastrously unsuccessful, motivating an even deeper retreat into geekhood."

I'M NOT ALONE, YOU'RE NOT ALONE

Piney Kahn, a fashionable chick with a definite nerdy side, runs a marketing collective in Portland, Oregon.

▶▶ "I think I've dated mostly geeks and nerds. At least, those are the ones that stuck. I've had a few pretty ones here and there, but pretty people are quickly boring, often one-dimensional, or are so self-involved that they often don't have interesting observations to share. They don't develop themselves and learn about things outside of themselves; they are too busy keeping up appearances. Geeks, on the other hand, gave up on appearances a long time ago and usually find self-acceptance. I prefer nerds and geeks because they can teach me new things and understand my odd frame of reference. And 'cause they get geeked out about the little things that I do."

Dr. Osborne cites studies that show that personality begins to take shape as early in life as 10 months. "This means parents and others begin to have an impact on our developing self-worth that early," he says. "The messages from books, television, and such begin to soak in at that point. If a myriad of our early exposures all show us that looking a certain way, doing a certain thing, valuing a certain thing gets positive responses from our significant caregivers—we notice that. If a toddler picks up a huge baseball bat and tries to swing it and the parents and others clap and cheer, that has an impact. Likewise, if the toddler wants to pick up a telescope or some other more 'intellectual' item and others do *not* react as positively, the toddler also notices that."

Finding Their Place in Society

No matter what, geeks and nerds have always been valuable to society, even if their peers made fun of them at the time. Look at Albert Einstein. It would be fair to say that he was one of the pioneering nerds. Not only was the man brilliant, but he also was so brilliant that he apparently didn't even have time to brush his hair. The name "Einstein" has become synonymous with "genius" in popular culture today, and good ol' Al has been the model for many a mad scientist or absent-minded professor. Even Yoda's (the *Star Wars* character, just in case you didn't know!) eyes were modeled after Einstein's. True story—character creator Nick Maley admits it in interviews.

History of the Word "Nerd"

The first use of the word nerd was by literary uber-dork Dr. Seuss in his 1950 story *If I Ran the Zoo*. Seuss's creature known as the Nerd even bore an uncanny resemblance to Einstein, with a crazy shock of white hair and a slightly grumpy look on his face. Woody Allen, Andy Warhol, Stephen Hawking, George Lucas, the band Weezer, Isaac Asimov, J.J. Abrams (the creator of *Lost* and monster movie *Cloverfield* and director of the *Star Trek* remake) and his horn-rimmed glasses, Steve Jobs, Bill Gates

. . . the list of nerds throughout history and in entertainment and pop culture goes on and on. Beaker and Dr. Bunsen Honeydew on *The Muppet Show*, Professor John I.Q. Nerdelbaum Frink Jr. on *The Simpsons*, Louis and Gilbert from *Revenge of the Nerds*, Gary and Wyatt in *Weird Science*, Harry Potter, Peter Parker (aka Spiderman), and Hiro Nakamura on *Heroes* are all beloved, fictional nerds. And even though traditionally nerds are known and defined as socially awkward and undesirable, they always seem to get the girls in movies. Hello, McLovin?

Are Nerds Almost Becoming . . . Desired?

So even though geeks and nerds may not have had society encouraging their intellectualism in the past, it seems times are changing. Yup, technology and science have saturated our culture, and we're seeing the rise of the Nintendo generation—kids who grew up on computers and video games in the 1980s and 1990s. The term normal has been redefined; the tables seem to be turning and society isn't laughing at nerds anymore. We want to join them, we want to get their super-smart inside jokes, and we want to type "pwned!" proudly when winning an Internet debate. And some us, well, just don't know how to go about doing all that. That's who this book is for.

Now, you might feel that you're having trouble getting over that "resistance hump"—the mental struggle that many a woman goes through when deciding to involve herself in her man's activities (*Am I changing to please a guy? Am I doing this for him or for me? And if I am doing this for him, does it make me a pushover?*). This actually is pretty serious, especially for a lot of women today who have been taught that they should never compromise themselves for a guy—that you're somehow sacrificing hard-earned independence and your own personality by "becoming the woman he wants."

To which I say: Get over it! He compromises for you—at least he should (any guy who doesn't is not worth it). He may have even found that he actually *likes* some of your stuff. And that's what good relationships are all about: sharing and caring. Aw, sappy.

10 Reasons to Love Geeks and Nerds

1. *They're sincere.* No frontin' here, that's for sure. What you see is what you get.
2. *They're sensitive.* Although their emotions most often get the best of them during, say, the end of *The Lord of the Rings: The Return of the King.*
3. *Geeks are usually one-woman men, meaning they're loyal.* A lot of times, geeks might be shocked that you're actually into them, or they might see you as a new and intriguing equation they must figure out. Either way, they shower you with attention—at least until it's time for gamescomicsanimecomputersiphoneetc. See "10 Things to Expect When You're Dating a Geek or Nerd" on page 8.
4. *They are considerate.* My boyfriend buys games with me in mind, games he thinks I might like to play with him.
5. *They're incredibly, hotly, wildly intelligent.* A high IQ is such a turn-on. I've dated geeky guys who might not have been traditionally handsome, but their skill sets and brains were so attractive that in my eyes, they were all Orlando Bloom.

6. *They're funny.* Sometimes you might not get their jokes; however, that's why you need to hone your skills. Then the next time your guy blurts out, "Do not want!" you can genuinely laugh in unison with him, instead of going, "Oh, ha ha!" and thinking, Do not want what?

7. *Your parents love them.* Mom was sick of your bringing home boy-men who, at age 30, are still chasing the dream of "Some day our band will make it!" Dad is impressed by your guy's credentials—he was a double major in physics and computer science, after all.

8. *He loves you most when you're wearing jeans, Converse, and no makeup.* As a matter of fact, he may claim it's his favorite outfit.

9. *Women are always complaining about how "men just want their bodies, and don't appreciate their minds."* Well, here's someone who values intelligence over physicality (not to say you're not hot, okay?).

10. *He fixes things.* Oftentimes, he sees this as a romantic gesture. Instead of roses, you might get a reconfigured hard drive. Sweet.

10 Things to Expect When You're Dating a Geek or Nerd

1. In the early stages of your relationship, it's best to communicate via e-mail or instant message. These forms of communication aren't as intimidating for geeks, who often feel that they articulate better via the written word than via actual, you know, speech.

2. He's efficient and focused. The following things will fall by the wayside when he is gaming/reading/programming:

a. Food. Geeks want something fast—if they even acknowledge their stomach rumbles—that's not going to "get in the way" of whatever they're currently working on. Slap a tray of Bagel Bites in front of him, and forget about it.

b. Showering. What's the point? No one can smell him online.

c. Communication. With you. I've totally gotten the hand wave before—the kind of hand wave I give him when I'm in the middle of watching *Law & Order*, the "Can't you see I'm doing something?" hand wave.

3. As intimidated as you are by his activities that you know nothing about, he's just as intimidated by yours. Try easing him into situations such as meeting all your girls for brunch by, say, just getting him out of the house on the weekends so he can see there are people actually walking around and talking. This leads me to number four . . .

4. Geeks and nerds often aren't too social (there are exceptions, and we'll look at them later). They're either shy or simply bored by most small talk, except when he is on his own turf or is surrounded by fellow geeks. Actually, even having one fellow geek around that he knows speaks his language will keep him from getting bored by the "mundanes" (that's normal human beings to you and me).

5. Interrupt an activity and get ready to have a cranky, downright angry geek on your hands. Never ask him to turn off a video game, get off the computer, put down a book/comic, or take off a costume. I'm sure you feel this way about some stuff too, right? It interrupts your flow,

and you're preoccupied with getting back to it—even if it's work.

6. You'll also have a cranky, downright angry geek on your hands if you don't let him participate in his activities enough hours (that's right, hours) during the week. Actually, forget I even used the words "let him." Ugh, are you his mom?

7. You must be direct. Geeks often are not up to speed on the nuances of conversation and are oftentimes very literal. Arguments may seem to go on for hours, with him spelling out his logical defense again and again: "You said we were leaving in an hour; by my estimate and the clock on the computer, I still had two minutes and fifteen seconds." Let him roll with it.

8. He's super analytical. That's just how his mind works—he's used to solving problems. He may read more into simple comments than you intend: "What exactly did you mean by 'Fine, then next time I won't invite you out'?"

9. He will freak out if you touch his stuff. Do not rearrange games because you think you're being sweet by alphabetizing them, do not even think of moving his computer because you want to dust around it, and, for god's sake, please do not pick something up and put it somewhere else. He has systems, and you're messing them up.

10. He may not be the most fashionable guy, unless you're dating an undercover geek, a type of geek becoming more and more common these days. Definition: These are the guys who, motivated by the promise of advancing their careers, moved from their small towns to bigger metropolises. Undercover geeks learn to interact properly with

humans, and become very social. You might even meet one at a (gasp!) bar. He'll be the guy wearing Nike Dunks, with a job in graphic design and an interest in mid-century furniture. He's witty and sarcastic and has lots of female friends. You might not even know you're dating a geek until, comfortable enough with you, he starts letting you see more and more of what he's really like: a goofy, lovable guy with an entire room full of toys in their original packaging.

Now onward future nerds in search of knowledge (and a greater understanding of your nerdy man).

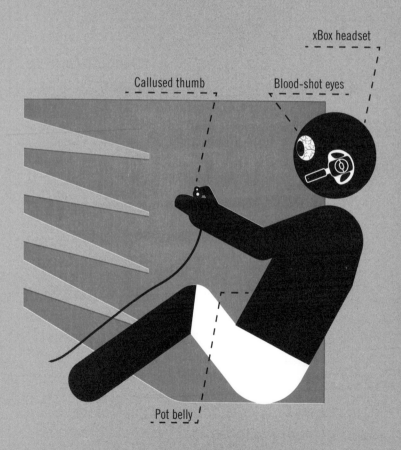

CHAPTER 2
"Can I just finish this level?"

Video Game Geeks

xBox headset

Callused thumb

Blood-shot eyes

Pot belly

In many relationships, the game controller is known as the mistress. She is always willing, always waiting, twenty-four hours, seven days a week. But she's a demanding mistress. Her siren song of intriguing, sometimes frustrating multiplayer games causes your man to block out all else: food, water, sunlight, you. But a word to the wise: The more you insist that your man not play video games, the more he wants to play them (this psychology is true of just about any restrictions you put on the typical male). He'll say you're "cramping his style."

Are You Jealous of the Game Controller?

This is how it used to be for my friend Kristin. Her boyfriend, Tom, was endearingly shy and socially awkward, to the point that Kristin had to explain his behavior to her friends: "No, he doesn't hate you, he's not a snob, he just doesn't get out too much!" She also knew that he liked to game. However, she thought his hobby was just that—a hobby. Her guy friends would say, "Oh yeah, I knocked out some Madden [*Madden NFL* games] this weekend," and she figured Tom was sort of along the same lines.

But all that changed when Kristin and Tom moved in together. You see, Tom was what is known as "the undercover gamer." Nervous that his obsession would cause a rift between him and Kristin, even though she'd pick up the controller with him every once in a while, he kept silent about just how much time he liked to spend gaming. It came as a shock to Kristin. "How can someone spend *six straight hours* shooting things and just *sitting* there?" she'd wail to her friends over the phone. "He doesn't even eat! He doesn't move. He doesn't talk!" In the background, machine gun fire could be heard. "And he wears this stupid, stupid, nerdy headset to talk to his friends on as he plays. It's like visual birth control, I tell you."

I'M NOT ALONE, YOU'RE NOT ALONE

Cailin Stamile, a young professional more into make-up than Madden, shares the tragic story of her man's transformation.

▶▶ "After an afternoon of lovin' with my husband, I ran out to take care of some errands. I came back to find my hubby sitting on the bed, wearing an Xbox headset, playing *Halo 3*, and yelling at his friends online. I scoffed at him, 'I left a man and came back to a boy!' And even though the headset is still in our home, I have no idea if he has ever worn it since that day, and I will never ask."

Facing the Facts

So obviously, there were a few issues. Kristin felt unhappy about asking Tom to stop doing something he loved so much, but she also felt slightly betrayed that Tom never let on how much he *really* loved it. When pressed about this, Tom was apologetic, but he still asked, "What did you think I meant when I said I gamed all weekend?" She felt like his mom. He felt guilty. And then came The Big Fight, which culminated in Kristin's accusing a bewildered Tom of "not understanding her."

Now, let's get something clear: We're talking about a great guy here. Tom works his ass off, he's beyond smart, and he treats Kristin as if she's a queen—when he's not gaming. And

Kristin knows all this. The day after The Big Fight, Tom cooked her breakfast. And Kristin—well, something inside her just snapped. In a good way. She realized that this was just who Tom was. And this was something he liked to do. Plus, she had to admit that he was always a good sport when she hosted *The Hills* marathons with her girlfriends.

So she took a deep breath. She picked up the still-unopened *LEGO Star Wars* game that Tom had bought so they could play together, and, well, sometimes I call her now and she says, "Can't talk. Leia and Luke in crisis. Stormtroopers attacking."

Kristin's not the only one who's been converted somewhat. Although law student Kerry isn't exactly what you'd call a "gamer" now, she does admit to playing a lot of the Tony Hawk games with her boyfriend, Joe, before they started dating—because it gave her an excuse to sit next to him for an extended period of time. Now, she sometimes plays *The Elder Scrolls IV: Oblivion* behind his back because, well, in the tradition of most alpha gamers, he tends to give too many annoying directions on how best to play the game when they're together.

Don't Ever Say, "It's Just a Game"

So why do geeks and nerds love games so much? It's all about a sense of challenge. There is a long-standing cliché that it's for the escapism, which really is secondary to the strong sense of accomplishment tied into games. He's handed challenges second by second, and if he overcomes them, he becomes "the man." A lot of nerds don't necessarily take well to physical challenges in the real world, so being able to jump rooftops in a game is pretty awesome. Also, with Xbox 360 and online role-playing games (RPGs—see terminology, page 22), he gets a sense of community—he can play with and against others, which gives him even more of a challenge. It's also one of the ways he keeps up with his friends. My boyfriend's closest friends live in Atlanta, Houston, and Brooklyn, but he meets all of them online every night for a game of *Call of Duty 4* or whatever multiplayer game they're into at the moment. Video game time is precious. Video game time recharges him. Think about what you like to do a whole lot, something that, when you're feeling down and out, lifts you up like no one's business and has you hopping around going, "Things are so great!" That's a game to guys.

Take Control of the Controller

Video games are actually *fun*. I swear. He may have tried to convert you with something terribly intimidating like *Resident Evil 4*, and after about five minutes of saying, "Do what now? Shoot where? How do I turn and shoot at the same time? Why am I *dying* again?" you probably flung down the controller in frustration. Getting good at anything takes time, and maybe you don't have it. That's why you have to start with the easy, girl-friendly games that let you get good after about three minutes of playing, and your character doesn't annoyingly die. I swear I'm not being condescending; I'm not saying that women don't like shooter games or sports games or anything with fast action. I know you like challenge and strategy. But once you get hooked on those, they'll get super boring. And eventually you'll be ready to move on to those first-person shooters, in which, perhaps, you can eventually kick your boyfriend's ass. Won't that be nice and satisfying? And really, you haven't heard true nerd pride until your man turns to his friend, beaming, and exclaims, "She can beat 'Rock You Like A Hurricane' on expert in *Guitar Hero 3!*"

Knowledge, Not M14 Shooting, Is Power

I'm not going to get into too many military-type games here (such as *Tom Clancy's Rainbow Six: Vegas*, *Call of Duty 4: Modern Warfare*, or the *SOCOM U.S. Navy Seals* games) simply because the only experience I have with these games is telling the BF to turn them the eff down. There's only so much M14 shooting I can take. I (and a lot of my girls who play games) find them pretty boring. But if you're into that kind of fighting, by all means, look into them.

I'm also not going to give you details on how to use any of the consoles or systems, because you're smart and that's why they make instructions. What I *am* going to do is help you have the most fun. But first, it's necessary to take a look at the history of gaming.

A Brief History

1972: The video game industry is firmly established with the creation of Atari Inc.

mid-1970s: The home market is born with a console called the Telstar by Coleco. In 1977, Atari comes to rule the market.

1979: Disgruntled Atari workers create Activision, the first independent video game developer to create games for all platforms.

1980: RPGs ramp up during the 1980s with computer games like *Zork*. Also, Nintendo releases the first handheld console, Game & Watch.

1982–1986: This is the golden age of arcade games, with pioneering games such as *Pong, Ozma Wars, Space Invaders, Galaga, Pac-Man, Pole Position, Donkey Kong, Joust*, and *Q*bert*.

1986: *The Legend of Zelda* debuts.

1987: *Final Fantasy* and *Metal Gear* debut.

1989: Nintendo releases the handheld Game Boy.

1992: Infamous RTS game *Dune II* sets the stage for future games such as *Warcraft: Orcs & Humans*.

1993: *Myst* becomes the best-selling game of the decade.

1994–1995: Sega releases Sega Saturn and Sony debuts PlayStation.

1996: FPS Internet game *Quake* pioneers Internet playing, and *Ultima Online* and *EverQuest* pave the way for MMORPGs such as *World Of Warcraft*.

1997: *Final Fantasy IV* sets the standard for RPGs.

1998: *The Legend of Zelda: Ocarina of Time* and *Metal Gear Solid* are released; both are widely considered among the greatest video games of all time.

2000: Sony releases PlayStation 2.

2001: Microsoft releases Xbox and its flagship game, *Halo*; Nintendo releases GameCube; Sega gets out of the hardware market and into third-party developing.

2004: The Nintendo DS handheld is released.

2005: Sony releases the PlayStation Portable (PSP) and Microsoft releases the Xbox 360; *Resident Evil 4* becomes the game of the year.

2006: Sony PlayStation 3 and Nintendo Wii are released.

2007: Microsoft unveils the Xbox 360 Elite, which includes high-definition video output and upgraded hard drive capacity; *Halo 3* is released and becomes the fastest selling video game in history.

Important Terminology

Boss: This is the huge enemy creature or challenge you have to beat to win a level or game. True bosses halt the game play until you defeat them.

Cheats/cheat codes: Also called "game guides," these are hints you can look up online that will help you play a game. Cheats are really for advanced levels. And they're not a cop-out! Everyone uses them.

Console: This is what you use to play the video game. It's usually connected to the television. You knew that.

Fail: Basically, this means to lose.

First-person shooter (**FPS**): This term refers to first-person action games that usually involve some sort of firearm or weapon. The player sees all the action through the character's eyes.

Leet/l33t speak: This is computer talk or "elite speak" that involves replacing letters with numbers that look like the letters. It's totally annoying, and most geeks I know hate it. Hackers used it a million years ago when bragging about their skills: "1337 h4x0rz pwn j00!" (Um, translation? "Godly hackers own you.")

Massively multiplayer online role-playing game (**MMORPG**): This is like your modern-day Dungeons & Dragons. You play with lots of people online, you have a definite story line, and you control a character who develops certain skills over a period of time. This is a commitment, baby, like *World of Warcraft*, and it's truly the ultimate nerd pastime when it comes to gaming. I know hard-core gamers who won't even get into this stuff. I also know hard-core MMORPGers who tell me, "Do not ever get into *WoW*. It's why I don't have a girlfriend—or a life."

N00b/newbie: Okay, these are two different things. A newbie is someone who is new to games and inexperienced. I was a newbie. A n00b, on the other hand, is someone who just flat out sucks and is ruining the game for everyone else. A n00b lacks common sense. Used in a sentence: "McGillicuddy, revive, you n00b!" Although, truth be told, n00b is played out.

Owned/pwned: Basically this means a player rules, as in "Hey, Boyfriend pwned you on this level!"

Platform game: This is just your regular, average video game, similar to an arcade game.

Role-playing game (RPG): In this time of game, you assume the role of a fictional character. A lot of times this is on a multiplayer level.

Story mode: You have to complete certain tasks or levels to get through the pre-defined story.

Third-person shooter (TPS): This is the general term for action games in which you can see the character. That is, you view the action as an observer controlling the character, not through the character's eyes.

World of Warcraft: One of the most well-known online RPGs, it was mocked/honored on the infamous *South Park* episode "World of Warcraft." The episode's a hilarious send-up and pretty true to life.

Special Pointers

1. Let your guy get you started on the game, but then get comfortable with the controls and setup, and try to play it by yourself as much as possible. I used to be sort of self-conscious with Mr. Gaming Expert watching me die over and over again, all the while saying, "You've got the right idea!" In gaming, that's kind of the equivalent of "Well, that's an interesting new haircut."

2. Play with other girls. At my office, we had a big flat-screen TV in the back room where my girls and I would play *Guitar Hero* after hours. One of them was better than I was, so she gave me pointers. The other one was a newbie, so

she made me unafraid of trying a harder level than what I was used to.

3. Please be sure to handle the games the same way you handle your DVDs, on the sides only. Not only do you not want to scratch them, but you really don't want your boyfriend scolding you about how you "abuse the games" and telling you to "please don't touch my stuff again." (Side note: Never "touch his stuff" without permission anyway. The games are all arranged a certain way, in a certain order, and disrupting the whole system is tantamount to disrupting his entire ordered world.)

4. At the advanced gaming level, you might want to read up on the games before you play them. I can give you the general idea here, but you'll want to know details of each game's plot (because a good portion of them are plot-based) so you'll know ahead of time what you are trying to accomplish and how to go about doing it.

5. You can save most games and your history playing them, so don't worry if you keep arriving at a point in the game that you can't get past or if you have to stop playing the game suddenly to, oh, I don't know, eat or something.

Getting to Know Your Games—Beginner Level

I'm going to break down the games by platform (that is, Nintendo Wii, Xbox 360, etc.), but keep in mind that most games are cross-platform, so if your geek doesn't have a certain console, more than likely the games I recommend can be played on something else.

What's the Deal with the DS?

Basically, Nintendo DS and DS Lite are the *biggest* little hand-held consoles in the world. What's the DS Lite? It's a lighter, thinner version of the Nintendo DS. What's the Nintendo DS? It's a small, portable game console that you can hold in your hands. And it's relatively cheap: about $130 at your local Kmart, Wal-Mart, Circuit City, or other big-box store. A lot of women get addicted to gaming thanks to the DS and DS Lite. I know that my games of *Puzzle Quest* last way, way past my bedtime. And I play them in bed because, yes, the DS is *portable*, so you can take it wherever: on the subway, on a long road trip, in bed, even under the desk at a super boring work meeting. Bonus: Your geek can't see what you're doing, so he can't try to take the controller out of your hands and tell you you're doing it wrong. Here are some games to get you started with the DS.

Puzzle Quest: Challenge of the Warlords

This game is a combination of RPG and puzzle-solving challenges. In a world full of knights, orcs, elves, dwarves, warriors, dungeons, and the like, you're off to save the world by solving puzzles against your enemies. Crack may be wack, but not if it's of the *Puzzle Quest* variety.

Mario Kart DS

This is any gamer's favorite racing game! You can race your fave Nintendo characters (don't have one yet? May I suggest cutie mushroom head Toad?) against one another in karts, and attempt to defeat your opponent by doing things like using the flying squid to shoot black ink on your competitors. If you have wireless Internet access, you also can exchange "friend codes" with your buddies and play against them online.

The Legend of Zelda: Phantom Hourglass

If you want something a bit more complicated than puzzle and racing games, try this Zelda game. Check out *The Legend of Zelda: Twilight Princess* under the Wii section of this chapter for the gist of Zelda games.

Nintendo Wii

The most girl-friendly console ever is the Nintendo Wii for several reasons: It doesn't feel as if you're playing a video game, the characters are so darn cute they'll make you want to squeeze their little cheeks, and it's super easy to use. I'm sure your geek already has one because he had to stand—er, sit—in line starting at 5 A.M. the morning they were released so he could have bragging rights. This will be true of all the game consoles, actually.

The Wii has two controllers called the Wii Remote and the Nunchuck, and you use real-life motions to play the games. For example, while playing Wii bowling, you actually stand up and swing your arm forward as if you were rolling a bowling ball in real life.

First, you'll want to make your own Wii character. This is the character you'll use to play certain Wii games. My BF and I made characters that looked like us, and then we got a little drunk and made a couple of characters that are basically weird aliens with huge heads, sunglasses, and nonsensical names.

Okay, I know, I know. That's why we're nerds. Anyway, Wii comes already loaded with *Wii Sports*, which lets you play tennis, bowling, golf, baseball, and boxing. These games are super fun and great to play at parties. You also can download this thing called the Everybody Votes Channel, which lets you vote on things like "What do you like better, hot weather or cold weather?" The Wii then compares your answers to the answers of other people all over the world. Sound simplistic? Wait until 3 A.M. on a Friday night, after you get home from your favorite bar.

Animal Crossing

This game is adorable and pointless, but beware: You will get sucked in so hard that you'll find yourself waking up at least an hour early in the morning so you can play.

The entire point of the game is to create a virtual "perfect town" within a world of animals. You start with nothing but a small house to live in and a job with the local general store run by Tom Nook (you'll have a love/hate relationship with him). You have to pay off your mortgage by working for Nook, but you can do other things to earn tons of money.

Sound too much like what you have to do in real life? Forget about that. In real life, you don't get to prance around your town wearing a gray beard, a crown, and a red cape and carrying a million bells (*Animal Crossing* speak for "dollars"). And you don't have neighbors like Lobo the wolf and Bluebear the bear coming up to you to spread gossip about other neighbors. You also can invent your own phrases, such as "Good morning, you bad MotherF'er!" and teach your neighbors how to say them.

The Legend Of Zelda: Twilight Princess

This is part of the famous *Legend Of Zelda* series that brought video games mainstream waaay back in the 1980s. If you already have even the slightest bit of nerd in you, this game will appeal to you because it's a—wait for it—*fantasy* game. It's cool on the Wii because you use the Wii Remote and the Nunchunk, which make it feel more interactive, of course. The main character, Link, is transported into the "Twilight" and attempts to pursue monsters that have kidnapped his friend. There's lots and lots going on here, so sometimes you'll forget what the whole point of the game is because you'll get caught up in doing other stuff, such as trying to heal your new friend Midna by finding the Master Sword that Princess Zelda clues him in on. Link can switch back and forth between human and wolf forms. There are a lot of crystals and swords and imp-characters, but if this still sounds a little convoluted to you, consider *Animal Crossing*.

Sony PlayStation 2

If your BF has an Xbox, the PS2 is probably collecting dust, so he won't care *what* you do to it. (That won't be true of his PlayStation 3, which he will be buying if only for the simple fact that you can watch Blu-ray discs on it.) Consider PS2 your practice platform. Sony probably won't produce too many more PS2 games because it's trying to push the PS3 platform.

Suikoden III

This game is an oldie, but a goodie. Kind of like a Choose Your Own Adventure novel, *Suikoden III* lets you experience the same storyline from three different perspectives. Each character can do different things in the game, building castles and collecting Stars of Destiny among them, and for some odd reason, you actually find yourself caring about Hugo, Geddoe, and Chris Lightfellow. Yes, I know it's geeky to care about imaginary video game characters, but that's why you're reading this book, right? It is, like Kingdom Hearts II (discussed next) an easy introduction into the world of RPGs.

Kingdom Hearts II

In this game, Disney characters try to find their missing buddies. It's kind of an RPG mixed with a regular platform game, so it's an easy introduction to RPGs. And when I say easy, I mean easy. You'll get lots of practice breezing through different worlds as the character Sora, who wields a powerful "keyblade" to destroy the heartless. Yeah for the powers of good! Since this is an RPG, you can customize certain abilities that your character has. You also can get through most of the game without dying, which, as we all know, is one of the biggest frustrations when first getting into gaming.

Microsoft Xbox 360

When you start to think about getting a 360, make sure you get one with online capabilities so you eventually can play live with your friends and other gamers; plus, you can download new game demos. Don't worry, your geek already has one.

Rock Band

If you're not the cutesy kind of girl, and *Cooking Mama* and *Animal Crossing* sound too precious for you, then you might want to try *Rock Band*. (There's also a PlayStation version.) This game is just flat out awesome, and I moved on to it after my *Guitar Hero* obsession (you might remember *Guitar Hero* as the game that Serena kicked Vanessa's ass on in *Gossip Girl*). *Rock Band* has these plastic guitar controllers that you use to, yes, play guitar to the songs on the game, *and* it has a whole mini drum set and microphone, as well! If, like me, you're jealous of anyone with musical talent, then *Rock Band* is your rock star fantasy. Sometimes when I'm playing Blue Öyster Cult's "Don't Fear the Reaper," I like to do these really big strumming motions like guitar legend Pete Townshend's.

There are four levels on *Rock Band*, just like on *Guitar Hero*—easy, medium, hard, and expert. You'll feel so accomplished once you master the easy level and can play through a whole song without making a mistake. Sometimes I'll kind of shake my hand out at the end of a song and say, "Whew, man, my fingers were on fire!" So far, I've mastered the bass, but drums are kicking my ass. I haven't tried vocals yet, but the fun thing about singing vocals is that during breaks in the song you're supposed to "freestyle," say something like, "Woooo, great to see you tonight, Chicago!"

You also get to create your band characters, outfit them, give them makeup, and even customize some tattoos for them. Naming your band is the most fun. Have you ever had dreams of playing for Pie or Donkey Punch? Go for it. You can tour the world, get a publicist and manager, gain fans, and earn cash. Trust me, you want to earn lots of cash so you can buy new clothes and accessories, such as a spiked armband and helmet, for your character. Seems realistic, right?

Dance Dance Revolution ULTRAMIX

Dance Dance Revolution ULTRAMIX is a game in which you attempt to follow the on-screen dancing by jumping on little pads you lay out on the floor. Get in shape and annoy your downstairs neighbors at the same time! What could be more fun?

Getting to Know Your Games—Moving Beyond Beginner

Okay, so you're done waking up at 5 A.M. to water your flowers on *Animal Crossing*, and your band is playing Bibliotheque Morte in Paris. At this level, since you've become comfortable with game controls and the general gist of games, try playing in co-op mode, which is when you and your man play together—not against each other. Then, if you get stuck at a certain point, you can have him pick up the slack (for now, at least, but pretty soon you'll be kicking his ass all over the place). It's also sort of bonding and, dare I say, romantic to play side by side. You're both working toward the same goal, and can support each other in your efforts. You might even start waking up on Saturdays looking forward to playing with your geek. You've been watching him play first-person shooter games, and if you're a fan of horror movies, some of them look downright scary and thrilling. So let's explore more options, shall we?

Nintendo Wii

Did you borrow your Wii when you were just a lowly beginner? Now that you're getting better at playing games, it might be time to consider buying one for yourself. Or, you know, just keep using your guy's.

Super Mario Galaxy

The Mario franchise will never die! This game follows Mario in his endeavors to save Princess Peach from his archenemy, Bowser. He travels through different galaxies and visits various planets to collect Power Stars. The coolest thing about this game is that each planet has its own "gravitational force," and you aren't limited to running around on a flat, two-dimensional surface. You can walk sideways and upside down, jump from planet to planet—it's almost like riding a roller coaster, I swear. If you want to ease into the game and get your geek excited at the same time, be all, "Hey, wanna play *Mario Galaxy* together tonight?" Then you can play in co-op Co-Star Mode. One of you plays Mario (he'll probably want to do this) while the other helps shoot Star Bits and stop enemies.

Metroid Prime 3: Corruption

Metroid Prime 3 follows the *Metroid Prime* storyline (don't worry, you don't really have to know too much of the backstory to play), with the Galactic Federation's network computers infected with a virus. The Federation thinks those dastardly Space Pirates are behind it, and contracts you, a bounty hunter named Samus Aran, to track them down and neutralize the virus before the whole galaxy is destroyed! The cool thing about this? Samus is a *girl*. Yup, you finally get to kick ass as your own gender.

Sony PlayStation 2

There also are some awesome, more advanced games that you can play using your (or your BF's, let's be honest) Sony PlayStation 2. Like these:

Okami

This is a visually beautiful game. Funny enough, it's also a really good segue into the world of manga and anime, which we will be exploring in Chapter 4. *Okami* is based on the Japanese legend of the sun goddess Amaterasu, the character you play throughout the game in the form of a white wolf. Since you've already played *Zelda*, you're familiar with the fantasy aspect of games like this. *Okami* is a bit more obtuse, since it relies heavily on Japanese folklore, but that's okay—you actually can *learn* stuff playing it.

Amaterasu holds the divine or celestial brush, which is quite literally a paintbrush that looks like Amaterasu's tail. You can use it to defeat enemies by painting simple shapes and lines that turn into "miracles." For instance, you can cut an enemy in half by painting a line through the center of him. It's a gentle, intelligent, almost artistic contrast to most of the testosterone-heavy games at this level, and Amaterasu is female. The graphics look almost like watercolor paintings, and the whole package has a sort of calming effect. Ahhhh. I can feel relaxed just talking about it, like a nice warm bubble bath.

Bully

Bully is a great game to get you into the whole RPG world. You play the role of fifteen-year-old Jimmy Hopkins, who's new to Bullworth Academy and trying to fit in with—or conversely, irritate—all the school cliques. It's kind of great revenge if you were hassled as a teen; you get to throw stink bombs, use your slingshot, play pranks on malicious kids, or be a malicious kid yourself, since Jimmy can get a little nasty at times. He can "learn" to kiss better in order to restore his health, opt to skip class or to attend (I won't tell you what you get if you attend class, but just remember, skipping school is bad!), and juggle plenty of girls, believe it or not. Personally, I like making sure that Jimmy stays unpopular with his jockish classmates. (*Bully: Scholarship Edition* is now on Xbox and Wii as well, so get one of those versions if you have the consoles.)

Microsoft Xbox 360

Once you've reached this level in your gaming development, you'll find yourself talking about things like "graphics" and enjoying the prospect of multiplayer games on your Xbox 360. You *have* created your Xbox 360 account, right? That'll be your "gamer tag." I'm going to throw in a couple of extra Xbox game suggestions for you, since you've worked so hard.

Viva Piñata

A good game to progress to on the Xbox, *Viva Piñata* is similar to *Animal Crossing* but more graphics driven and a bit more complicated, and it involves piñata animals that you can breed and care for. You also have to fend off enemies in this game, unlike in *Animal Crossing*. The enemies will eat your nice piñatas, and that tends to make me super sad.

LEGO Stars Wars II: The Original Trilogy

Here's something a bit more challenging. This game appeals to women because the characters are so friggin' cute—don't make fun! They're made out of LEGO bricks and, obviously, represent characters in the *Star Wars* franchise, such as Luke Skywalker, Princess Leia, and Han Solo. If Episodes I, II, and III were more your speed, then by all means, pick up the *LEGO Stars Wars* versions of those instead.

You can adjust the difficulty level in this game, and you also can play co-op. The objective is to get to LEGO City level, but honestly, the game's so fun to play that you forget all about where you're supposed to be going. If you are *any* kind of *Star Wars* fan, then this will bring out the kid in you. Never been that into *Star Wars*? Try *LEGO Indiana Jones*—different movie, still cool.

Grand Theft Auto IV

The *Grand Theft Auto* series is one of the most infamous game series in the world. Film veterans such as Michael Madsen, Samuel L. Jackson, James Woods, Joe Pantoliano, Frank Vincent, Robert Loggia, and Ray Liotta all have voiced major characters. Basically, you take on the role of a criminal in a major city, and have the opportunity to rise through the ranks of organized crime by completing tasks to advance to each level, all while driving super fast through the city. What is cool about this series is that the player has *a lot* of freedom to pick and choose what she wants to do in the game (geeks call this type of game a "sandbox game"). Your relationship with other characters in the game changes based on what tasks you choose to take on. There also are "radio stations" that you can listen to while driving. Other games in this series are:

- *Grant Theft Auto, Grand Theft Auto 2, Grand Theft Auto III*
- *Grand Theft Auto: Vice City*
- *Grand Theft Auto: San Andreas*
- *Grand Theft Auto: Liberty City Stories*
- *Grand Theft Auto: Vice City Stories*

Phew. That's a lot. You can play any of these games to get started; you don't have to follow the series, although it's fun to see some of the inside jokes that run throughout all the games.

This series is fun for two simple reasons: You get to drive really, really fast and do illegal things that make you feel slightly dangerous. If you're a law-abiding lady and the idea of illicit activity makes you feel sort of uncomfortable, but you still like the action and aggression, then try some first-person shooters. You might want to look into the *Halo* series or *The Orange Box*. Every geek I know can't say enough good things about *The Orange Box*, which is actually five games in one. *Portal* is an FPS/puzzle type game, so try starting with this one.

BioShock

Playing *BioShock* is almost like watching a movie you can interact with. As a matter of fact, the plot is so detailed and interesting that you should read up on it before you start to play. It's scary, too, and has a "morality based" story line, which means that you're basically working for a greater good and are allowed to make "good" choices or "evil" choices. The game has different endings depending upon the player's decisions. The plot follows a plane crash survivor named Jack, who must explore the underwater-utopian-society-gone-very-wrong Rapture. There are genetically mutated folks roaming around (the Splicers, who jump out at you from seemingly nowhere) and these huge creatures called Big Daddys that act as guardians to evil little girls called Little Sisters. You have two choices for dealing with the Little Sisters: You can "harvest," or kill, them, or you can save them. Think hard about the decisions you make and their possible effects!

What Have We Learned?

- By definition, "games" are supposed to be fun—and these games are fun!
- The Xbox headset still is the nerdiest thing ever, even if you do wear it on occasion. Welcome to the club of nerd-dom.
- "Beyond beginner" games often have story lines that are as detailed as a novel's, so it's fun to read up on them.
- It's easy to coordinate your frustrations with your game. Have road rage? Play *Grand Theft Auto*. Idiotic co-workers

who move too slow? Shoot zombies in *Resident Evil 4*. Your boss humiliated you in front of said co-workers? Kill some Big Daddys in *BioShock*.

- "GamerGrrrl" is not a good Xbox tag, unless you want to be hit on constantly by sixteen-year-olds.

Comic Book and Graphic Novel Geeks

Ponytail and goatee

Vintage Captain America t-shirt

List of Wednesday releases

Wednesday Releases

Warren Ellis Novel Signing

Line ticket for Warren Ellis signing

Squee

Cat named 'Squee'

Ah, the comic book store. That dark, cavernous place your geek disappears into every weekend. You go with him, kind of stand around the front as he eagerly attacks the new issues of *Ultimate X-Men*, and aimlessly flip through whatever they have by the cash register. Your geek comes up to you and says in a hushed whisper, "Just a few more minutes; I have to go look upstairs—back soon." And there he goes, loping off into the gloom, not to be seen for another half hour.

The Great Beyond, Finding Your Way

You sigh. Okay, maybe you should look around, just to kill time. Hmm, where to start? You walk the aisles, feeling slightly self-conscious. Guys line the Marvel and DC section, and you take a peek—but good god, there are fifty versions of *Batman*, *X-Men*, *Spider-Man*, and *Superman* all the way up to the ceiling. Okay, so maybe not this aisle.

You take a look at another aisle that's just as confusing because it seems that there's stuff in there you recognize, but the way it's filed makes no sense. You pick up *Sandman* but notice it's volume 2. That won't do. You look around nervously, trying to avoid Comic Book Store Guy and his haughty "Do you need any *help*?" You feel like a total dorky neophyte with one of the best-known comics in your hand. You put it back on the shelf like a hot potato. You realize that you have no idea which one of these volumes or collections or issues or whatever is actually *good*. When you take your purchases to the counter, will Comic Book Store Guy curl his lip and silently judge you? Who cares, right? You care. You actually really do.

I'M NOT ALONE, YOU'RE NOT ALONE

Cat Kinney, a former comic book store employee, is a proud nerd.

▶▶ "We had one guy when I first started working there who considered himself an intellectual and who dissed anyone who deigned to read Marvel's mutant titles or Image anything. He only bought very particular independent titles and loved The Comics Journal, which I find erudite and condescending. I think my presence softened the terror for some women, as I was an enthusiastic helper to anyone who had questions. If they picked up something that they liked or thought was cute, I would happily chat with them about it and ring them up. I really tried to make other women feel welcome there, as we were a definite minority back then. I think the thing that is even more terrifying to customers than the mockery of the comic shop employee is the employee's relative possession of weak social skills. All of us had shortcomings, and most of us were aware of them."

The aisles start closing in on you, all these comics, all these graphic novels, toys, playing cards, superheroes, monsters . . . must . . . get . . . out . . . you grab *Sandman* volumes 2, 4, and 6 and head for the counter. That's when you see him. Comic Book Store Guy.

He's apparently had it with the plebian customers on the floor and now sits very high on his throne behind the cash register. You clear your throat. His head turns. He looks down at you. And slowly, soooo slowly, his lip curls and he silently judges you. And then you wake up.

Back to Reality

Okay, so maybe this is over-dramatized a bit, but it's how a lot of women who are comic newbies feel when they go into a comic book store, normally a shadowy realm inhabited only by guys and Goths (yes, they still exist, and they're in the horror aisle). The stereotype of the judgmental comic book store clerk is so pervasive (thank Jeff Albertson, aka Comic Book Guy, on *The Simpsons*) that it's easy to feel intimidated.

So, the employee you think is going to judge you for picking up a random issue of *Batman* just because you know who Batman is probably (a) is a person who really wants to help you, because he enjoys comics and wants to spread the love or (b) is unskilled with social nuances and uses his knowledge as armor. Sort of like your very own nerd, right?

What's His Reasoning?

So why does your nerd like comics? Well, guys are fans for different reasons. And of course, as with anything else, there are varying degrees of fans. We're going to stick with the basics here. If you want to know more about uber-geeky stuff like cosplay (dressing up in costumes and acting as a certain character), you can read about that in Chapter 4.

Basically, guys like comics because "the idea of other worlds and people with fantastic gifts or powers is exhilarating," says Jimmy Aquino, sketch comedy writer/performer and esteemed co-host of *Comic News Insider* (*CNI*), one of the most well-known comic-book-and-all-things-nerdy podcasts. On *CNI*, Jimmy and his partner, Joe Gonzalez, host a segment called "Converting to

Comicdom," during which women read a couple of comics and review them on air honestly. Sometimes Jimmy even asks them to do "homework" by visiting a comic store.

Want to know another reason why nerds and geeks like comics? It's like debate club all over again, and now you can never win or lose! They like to argue, continuing to assert their superior intelligence over their opponents. If you haven't heard the Batman vs. whomever or Marvel vs. DC debate at least once, you might not be dating a *true* comic nerd.

So You Mean It's Not Kids' Stuff?

So why should *you* like comics? Do you get a warm sense of nostalgia when seeing movies like *Spider-Man*, *Batman Begins*, or *Transformers*? Do the touches of romance in these films appeal to you? Maybe you still watch shows like Cartoon Network's *Adult Swim*, cartoons that definitely are not for your eight-year-old cousin. Just like these shows and movies, comics take you back to your old, childishly enthusiastic self, before adult ennui set in.

Then again, maybe you weren't the cartoon or superhero type. But you had to have other interests. Film, perhaps? When I read a comic, it's like a running film in my head. Reading a comic by a good artist, I can almost see the action and feel the emotion. Be sure to check out pointer number two in the Special Pointers of this chapter, where I outline how to match your interest to the appropriate comic genre.

I'M NOT ALONE, YOU'RE NOT ALONE

Raph (like Teenage Mutant Ninja Turtle bad-boy Raph) Soohoo hosts the podcast *Geeks Unite!* and works at one of the largest comic book stores in Manhattan.

▶▶ "Most women would think comics are for kids, they're silly, or they're violent. Well, they are, but that's just one aspect. Most people tend to associate superheroes with comics, but comic books are not books with superheroes. Comic books are a medium. Comics are probably one of the most powerful, evocative mediums in existence. The point of being a fan shouldn't be tearing apart people's work or complaining or only talking to others in the know. It's about sharing what you love."

Graphic Novels—Comics' Bigger Brother

You also might hear your geek talk about graphic novels. Some people think that the term *graphic novel* is a more sophisticated way to refer to comics. Wrong! Graphic novels are bound soft-covered books that consist of a complete story; they're like a novel with pictures. Graphic novels are not trade paperbacks, which look like graphic novels but are actually collections of comic book issues re-released in book format.

Comic-Con—The Bane of Your Existence or Potential Fun?

Does your nerd or geek sneak off for a "boys weekend" every summer? Does he disappear with a suspiciously bulging duffle bag and return with smears of red or green or purple on his collar? Relax. He's not cheating on you with a punk rock dominatrix. He's just been at Comic-Con.

Comic-Con International, held in San Diego, is one of the largest comic book conventions in the world. You can thank a guy named Shel Dorf and a few of his fellow San Diegans for coming up with the brilliant idea that holds your geek hostage every year.

In 1970, Dorf founded the Golden State Comic Book Convention, which eventually became Comic-Con. The convention is almost sensory overload for your geek—and guaranteed to cause a meltdown in any non-geek. It's a four-day event with a special preview night that brings together comic dealers, collectors, TV networks, and film studios all exhibiting their wares. There also are panels featuring *big* names in the comic industry (such as the godfather of comics, Stan Lee) as well as film and television (like Rosario Dawson and Samuel L. Jackson). You're likely to see special previews of upcoming films that have something to do with comics. There are exclusive toys to be bought (holographic Princess Leia! Spawn the Bloodaxe San Diego exclusive 6″ action figure Spawn Dark Ages: series 22!), autographs to be had in the special autograph area (Kristin Chenoweth puts pen to paper!), and pictures to be taken with hot cosplay girls (beware any and all Japanese maids). Your geek probably doesn't do that last one because he's got *you*, but this is one of the few opportunities that many con attendees have to get close to a real, live girl.

Are you overwhelmed yet? Well, there's also Masquerade, where cosplayers get up on stage and perform skits for prizes, and portfolio reviews by industry professionals (picture 4,000 people screaming in delight at onstage ninjas battling pirates to a soundtrack of Dir en Grey). Comic-Con has become so popular over the years that it's branched out into manga, anime, and video games (servicing all your nerd and geek needs, right in one spot!).

What You Need to Know to Get Through a Comic-Con

So maybe your man doesn't sneak off every year with his costume in a duffle bag and come back with his makeup all over his clothes, but if he's interested in comics he has definitely attended at least once in his life. Comic book conventions are held in other cities (most notably New York, which is catching up to San Diego), and there are smaller cons like WonderCon and Alternative Press Expo.

Chances are *you* might be attending a con of some sort at some point. Here are some helpful tips to get through it and possibly even *enjoy* it:

1. Walk the convention floor and people watch. There will be tons of ridiculous costumes, but if you laugh, be prepared for the costume wearer to come over and harass you by pretending to behead you with his lightsaber or something.
2. Go check out the panels! There's bound to be someone you've heard of speaking on one. It's kind of cool to hear J.J. Abrams talk about his co-creation *Lost*, live and in person. It just adds to the fun when the fanboys start grilling him: "So, in episode number seventy-eight, I noticed that

there was a tree in one shot, but when you cut away and then went back, there was no tree. Was this intentional and if so, what is the symbolism?"

3. In that regard, check out the movie previews or the independent films in the film room.

4. Like getting attention? Think your geek or nerd is the type to do the whole "Yeah, she's with me"/chuckle thing? Then dress in costume. You will have guys lining up to take your picture. Just be sure to wear something substantial under your skirt (not a thong), because you don't want to wind up on YouTube as the subject of "Girls of Comic-Con Up Skirt" videos.

5. Go to Masquerade and laugh at the furries with everyone else. Don't know what furries are? They are people who dress up in animal costumes and take it very seriously. They apply sexy human characteristics to animals, and sometimes they do dirty things in their animal suits. At Comic-Con you may hear them referred to as "furverts."

A Brief History of Comics

There is *so much* that has gone on in the history of comics. We'll just focus on some of the biggies.

1933: *Famous Funnies*, considered by historians to be the first "true comic book," is published.

1934: DC Comics, one of the main comic book publishers, is founded under the name National Allied Publications.

1938: Superman is introduced to an unsuspecting public. *The Man of Steel* was an instant hit, of course. Fun fact: Did you know that Nicolas Cage named his son Kal-el after Superman's birth name?

Approximately 1938: The golden age of comics begins.

1939: Marvel Comics, one of the main comic book publishers, is founded as Timely Publications.

1939: Batman is introduced. Unlike most superheroes, he doesn't have "super powers"; he fights his war on crime with his smarts and technology, just like our beloved geeks.

1940: The comic strip *Brenda Starr* debuts. It was the first notable comic created by a woman, Dale Messick.

1941: DC introduces Wonder Woman. She was designed by psychiatrist William Marston to embody the ideals of female heroism. Archie Andrews of the Archie Comics also debuts.

1950: Good grief, Charlie Brown. Charles Schulz creates *Peanuts*, the most profitable comic strip of all time.

Approximately late 1950s: The silver age of comics begins.

1962: Spider-Man and the Hulk are introduced. Peter Parker, Spider-Man's alter ego, is a total nerd.

1963: Mutant fighters the X-Men debut. They go on to become one of the biggest franchises in comic books.

Approximately mid-1970s: The bronze age of comics begins.

1973: Howard the Duck debuts along with a bunch of strong female characters such as Spider-Woman, She-Hulk, and Red Sonja.

Approximately mid-1980s: The modern age of comics begins.

1984–1985: Spider-Man gets his black costume.

1986: Art Spiegelman creates *Maus*. Based on his father's Holocaust experiences, this graphic novel goes on to win a special Pulitzer Prize in its collected form. *Maus* helps raise the respectability of graphic novels.

1992: *Spawn*, a character and comic created by Todd McFarlane, debuts. In 1994, McFarlane forms McFarlane Toys, one of the most well-known contemporary toy companies.

Late 1990s–2000s: Trade paperbacks boom and, in a way, help to save the flagging comic industry, which had seen a drop in sales. People become more interested in comics because they don't have to buy fifty or more small issues to catch up on a story; they can buy just half a dozen books.

Comic Book "Ages"

Comic books are broken into different eras, or "ages." These are pretty much all about the superheroes. Even if you think superheroes are for little kids, this timeline is a good indication of how comics have become more sophisticated as a whole. Now, there are lots of plot-driven, gorgeously drawn books.

The Platinum Age

Generally, this refers to anything published before 1938. For example, in 1933, salesman Maxwell Gaines and sales manager Harry I. Wildenberg collaborated on *Famous Funnies*, published by Dell. This is considered by many historians to be the first *true* comic book. Of course, the art of comics has existed for centuries—even hieroglyphics were a form of communication that used pictures to portray a message.

So why was 1938 the cutoff point for this era, you ask? As I point out in "A Brief History of Comics," that's when Superman was created. This ushered in . . .

The Golden Age (1938 to the mid-1950s)

The golden age of comics also could be called the superhero age. This is when the concept of a superhero was really defined, and some of the most famous superheroes were introduced during this period. Over time, superheroes got more sophisticated and started to develop personalities and run into conflict.

The Silver Age (late 1950s to early 1970s)

Superheroes were declining in popularity. There was a rise in horror and crime comics. Maybe people lost faith in "happily ever after" following World War II, the Korean War, and Vietnam. In any case, comic publishers DC and Marvel went head to head trying to outdo each other with the Justice League of America and the Fantastic Four, respectively. Also, comic book artists started to experiment with different styles, such as surrealism and graphic design elements, which leads us to . . .

The Bronze Age (1970s and 1980s)

The story lines were more mature and even included stuff you wouldn't want your six-year-old reading about. Horror-oriented titles such as *Swamp Thing* started to grow. Non-superhero titles became popular. Some people say the bronze age never ended, but others think we're in . . .

The Modern Age (mid-1980s to present)

This represents the "mainstreaming" of comics with dark and complex characters. Independent comics have flourished, and publishing houses have become more commercialized. The influence certainly can be seen in film and television, and has helped make a love of comics more acceptable to the mainstream.

Important Terminology

Book: short for comic book

Cameo appearance: when a character makes a quick, one-time guest appearance in a book

Complete run: *all* of the issues in a series (That is, if there are 250 issues and you have all of them, you have a complete run.)

Con: short for "convention"

Crossover: when a character appears in another comic book or story line

Dark age/iron age/diamond age: other names for the "modern age" of comic books

Debut appearance: the first appearance of a particular character

Fanboy: The fanboy exists across the board in gaming, films, sports, etc. But fanboys/girls mostly have been typified as the rabid, obsessive comic book fans who have arguments like "They were fighting at super speed, I tell you!" or are intense about continuity and details and always seem to think that they could "do it better"—whatever "it" may be.

Inker: the artist who does the "inking" for the art in comic books—or, more simply, the artist who applies the colors to the drawings the penciler (see below) has done

Key issue: something extraordinary or unique that has happened in a comic, such as when a main character made a debut appearance

Manga: simply, Japanese comics, but so much more than that (see Chapter 4)

Mutant: a mutated life form exhibiting super-human qualities

Panel: an individual frame in a comic

Pedigree: a certain status given to high-grade comic collections or books

Penciler: someone who draws the art for a comic in black in white (inkers fill in the colors)

Publisher: The two big publishers are DC and Marvel. There are numerous, loud, drawn-out, nitpicky debates on which one is better. This usually involves debating superheroes. See "fanboy." Other examples of well-known publishers are Archie Comics, which publishes the famous *Archie* series, and Dark Horse Comics, a successful independent that publishes stuff like *Aliens* and *Hellboy*.

Splash page: the first page of a comic book, usually with a big introductory illustration

Word balloon: the container that holds a character's dialogue (also "thought balloon")

Special Pointers

1. Remember what I said at the beginning of this chapter, and don't even worry about being intimidated in a comic book store. The last time I went to Forbidden Planet here in New York City, I had not one but three very nice salespeople ask me if I needed help or if I was looking for anything special—and not in a sarcastic way, either. At the very least, judgmental Comic Book Store Guy is probably just thrilled to have a cute woman enter his store.

2. When choosing a comic, think about what kinds of movies or television shows you like. There is a pretty good correlation to comics. Won't watch a film that's not on the Independent Film Channel? Frequent your local art museums? Independent comics or comics with detailed artwork are for you. Are you a big George Romero fan and into blood and guts? Horror all the way. Think *Law & Order* is the best show on TV? Go for crime comics. Do you consider yourself a strong female and like reading about other strong females? Did you like *Buffy the Vampire Slayer*? Although there are comics with strong female characters, you also might like some superhero stuff. I encourage you to check it out and try to knock that stereotype of "women don't like superheroes" on its ass. Are you more of the "laughing is therapy" persuasion? Comic authors

have great senses of humor and fill their books with jokes and references that even a novice would chuckle at. As a matter of fact, the more you go into certain series with a tongue-in-cheek attitude, the more you'll enjoy them. It's called suspension of disbelief, 'cause we all know that our next door neighbor doesn't secretly go into his basement and emerge a crime fighter in a bat costume.

3. Don't touch his collection. You've heard it before, but this pointer especially holds true for comics. You might not see the harm in taking one out of its Mylar sleeve to read it, and you might even think that he'll be charmed by your interest. He won't be. All he'll see are your fingers, perhaps wet with nail polish, smudging and creasing up the pages.

4. Go online and listen to my fave podcast, *Comic News Insider*. Although the entire show is informative and the hosts have amazing guests, the aforementioned "Converting to Comicdom" segment may pique your interest first. The results are always hilarious and surprising, with women asking some really good questions about the role of the subversive, disposable female characters in some comics. Often, and to their surprise, the girls find out that there are actually comics they like.

5. Most comic books are published monthly. Keep this in mind once you're hooked and trying to figure out when the next issue will be released. Though, the easiest way to read comics now is to get the trade paperbacks.

Getting to Know Different Genres—Beginner Level

There are so many different genres of comics! Remember pointer number two? I'm going to assign some comics to each of your possible interests to show you that there's more to comic life than heroes wearing capes and tights.

Artsy

Ghost World, story and art by Daniel Clowes

Tell people who think *Ghost World* is too mainstream to suck it and pick it up right away. If you haven't seen the movie (and after you read this, you should), you should know that the graphic novel is about two disaffected teenage girls, Enid and Rebecca, who aimlessly wander around their neighborhood in that "it's summer and we don't have anything better to do" way and spout hilarious, blackly comedic takes on people in their town, pop culture, and what they'll do for the rest of their days. In the opening pages, Enid and Becky comment on nerdy comedian Joey McCobb by saying, "What a loser." Pause. "I want to do him!" If you were even marginally discontent in high school and got annoyed when everyone else "discovered" Sonic Youth, you will relate. And laugh. And admire Enid's haircut.

Fell, story by Warren Ellis, art by Ben Templesmith

This easily could be thrown into the crime section; the reason it's included here is because, simply put, the art is beautiful. Illustrated by Ben Templesmith, one of the guys who worked on the *30 Days of Night* comic, it's delicate yet oppressive, realistic yet completely fantastical. Detective Richard Fell has been transferred to Snowtown, a place that puts *Se7ven*'s depressing, violent city to shame. Riddled with crime and unstable residents, at times *Fell* can feel formulaic and trite, but it's a short book and an easy read, and you can pick up any issue and jump right into the story. At the very least, you'll love examining the artwork. Pick up *Fell*, issue 3; it's the most cohesive, and the characters are better formed.

Horror/Crime

Sandman, story by Neil Gaiman, illustrated and inked by various people depending on the issue

I don't know if I should classify this as "horror" or "crime," but it's kind of a mix of horror, crime, and fantasy. *The Sandman* was a comic published in the 1970s about a superhero who was the master of dreams and protected kids from nightmares. Neil Gaiman came around in 1989 and gave good ol' Mr. Sandman a *totally* different edge. The main character, Morpheus, the King of Dreams, has been captured and imprisoned for 75 years. Once he escapes, he has to rebuild his kingdom. Start with *Preludes and Nocturnes*, volume 1, and then go from there. You also can get the 600-page anthologies, but they're expensive and a lot to swallow at first sitting. If you happen to have an embarrassing Goth past, *Sandman* will be that much more appealing. Morpheus is a romantic, conflicted, almost feminine character who looks like Nick Cave, and you might recognize a bit of yourself in the disenchanted, sarcastic character of Death.

Hellblazer, initially created by writer Jamie Delano and artist John Ridgway, though many others, including Warren Ellis and Garth Ennis, have worked on the series through the years

I bet you went to see *Constantine* in the theaters, even if it was just for star Keanu Reeves in a dapper suit. The movie's based on this comic series. The main character, John Constantine, has been around since the 1980s, when creator Alan Moore (also the writer of *Watchmen,* which you should check out if you're into dystopian and metafiction stuff) was writing for *Swamp Thing.* With *Hellblazer,* we're introduced to a more complex character, a guy of questionable morals who manipulates and deceives for the "greater good" of fighting powerful supernatural enemies. Cynical and reckless, he's a definite antihero who lives on the adrenaline rush of danger. Sadly, this always seems to backfire, and friends perish at the hands of his recklessness. Try the trade paperback *Hellblazer: Original Sins.*

Strong Females and Superheroes

ElfQuest, story and art by Wendy and Richard Pini

This is a comic book about elves. How much more nerdy can you get? *ElfQuest* originated in the 1970s, and I was *obsessed.* Even now, I hear lots of women admit to being fans of *ElfQuest,* and I've even had discussions that start like this: "Okay, which character did you want to be? Which one did you have a crush on?" I have to say, there are some pretty good themes in there about family and independence and how you need to be accepting of change. The community of elves, trolls, and other characters is just tryin' to get by, man. Most of the female elves in the story totally kick ass, hunting alongside their "lifemates," tanning animal hides, and in general acting as the "voices of reason" behind the males' impulsive actions—sort of how it is in real life, minus the hunting and tanning part. Warp Graphics, Wendy and Richard Pini's company that published *ElfQuest*, entered into a licensing agreement with DC Comics in 2003. This paved the way for the *ElfQuest* archives. You should start with *ElfQuest: Wolfrider*, volume 1.

Buffy the Vampire Slayer: The Long Way Home, story by Joss Whedon (director, creator, and producer of the Buffy TV series and lots more—see Chapter 5), art by Georges Jeanty

This is the comic book continuation of the seventh season of *Buffy the Vampire Slayer*, which aired on television. Talk about your strong females and heroines. Along with her sister, Dawn, who can transform into a giant, Buffy Summers leads a whole squad of powerful Slayers over in Scotland. If you were sad when the TV series ended, be sad no more. Sometimes when I'm in the gym and sure no one is watching me, I'll give one of the punching bags a little Slayer-esque kick. Buffy kinda makes you want to do that. If you want the whole experience, pick up *Buffy the Vampire Slayer Omnibus*, volume 1. If you just want a continuation of the TV series, get *Buffy the Vampire Slayer: The Long Way Home*.

Black Comedy/Satire

Strangers in Paradise, story and art by Terry Moore

Cat Kenney, the former comic book store employee whom we heard from earlier in this chapter, recommended this book. A comic for women who don't read comics, it easily could have been filed in the "artsy" category, as the drawings are so detailed, or the "strong female" category, since the two main characters are, er, females. But *Strangers in Paradise* also is random and hilarious (not to mention complicated and heartbreaking), revolving around the relationship between best friends Francine and Katchoo and the strange love rectangle, I guess, between them and their friends David and Casey. One minute you're empathizing with Francine's confused musings on growing up and being a woman, the next you're laughing at a common situation we've *all* experienced: waiting for a phone call, glaring at the phone, and, finally out of frustration, screaming: "RING!" *Strangers in Paradise* is nonlinear and unconventional; there's poetry, there's sheet music, and there's a plot to infiltrate and control the American political system. Terry Moore, the creator, also wrote for *Birds of Prey*, issues 47 to 49. If you didn't know better, you'd think Terry was a "she" not a "he" because he handles his female characters so adeptly. (Was he spying on my conversations with my best friend?) Start with the graphic novel *Strangers in Paradise*, issue 1.

Lenore, story and art by Roman Dirge

Roman Dirge is one of my favorite comic book creators, not only because of his style but because he shares that morbid, black humor so many ex- or closeted Goths love. *Lenore* is a hilarious, subversive take on pop culture and children's icons. Ten-year-old Lenore (known as "the cute little dead girl") lives in a mansion with all her friends, including Mr. Gosh (a dead person with a bag over his head) and Taxidermy (a man with the head of an embalmed deer). At first, Lenore is introduced as somewhat malicious, killing people out of spite, but in time she evolves into a lovable, bumbling character who *accidentally* kills people, even though she thinks she's doing good. It's really not as violent as it sounds—it's actually really adorable. (Am I twisted?) Start with the trade *Lenore: Noogies* for issues 1 through 4.

Getting to Know Different Genres—Moving Beyond Beginner

You're hooked! Right? Let's say you've already plowed though the stacks of beginner recommendations, to the point that even your geek is starting to ask, "Uh, you wanna, like, get out of the house or something?" Hey, who needs a social life when you've got all these new titles to check out? Onward, little soldier!

Artsy

Maus: A Survivors Tale, story and art by Art Spiegelman

Maus is the true story of narrator "Artie" and his father "Vladek." A survivor of the Holocaust, Vladek tells tales of life in Poland before and after World War II. Many of the characters are presented as talking animals; for example, Germans are portrayed as cats, and Jews as mice (hence the title *Maus*). Artie has a complex and somewhat troubled relationship with his father, who is very difficult to get along with. Considering that Vladek spent time in Auschwitz, that's not surprising. *Maus* won a special Pulitzer Prize award in 1992. Pretty impressive for a graphic novel.

Fun Home: A Family Tragicomic, story and art by Alison Bechdel

Fun Home, which takes place in the funeral home where Alison Bechdel and her family worked, was named one of the best books of 2006 by both *Time* and *New York* magazines. It's a beautiful graphic novel, and although the art isn't as refined as, say, the art in *Fell*, the story is incredibly personal and, at one point, moved me to tears. It's Bechdel's memoir, the tale of her family (particularly her father and his death) and her coming out as a lesbian. The interweaving of those aspects of her life, their causes and effects, and the parallels that are constantly drawn to classic literature and the role it played in Bechdel's and her father's lives are simple in their statements yet complicated in their meanings. Since it's a graphic novel, it is a fast read and something that you won't be able to put down until you're through.

Horror/Crime

The Walking Dead: Days Gone Bye, story by Robert Kirkman, art by Tony Moore (Charlie Adlard later replaced Moore)

Zombies! Gotta love 'em. Your geek certainly does. Although there are numerous zombie comics around, *The Walking Dead* earns significant praise. Depending on your scare threshold, this actually could be a comic that you would not want to read on a proverbial dark and stormy night, alone in your apartment. Cop Rick Grimes awakens from a coma to find the world filled with flesh-eating zombies. The comic's about his struggle to survive and ultimately boils down to a bit more than just zombies crunching on limbs—there's some social commentary on human nature, how people react in times of crisis, and what effect the crisis and their reaction to it would have on their future. (Essentially, the book's like a lot of zombie films, but we'll save that discussion for Chapter 5.) There's no political agenda here, though. The happenings are presented as fact, and even though you may disagree with certain decisions that the surviving humans make, just think about how *you* might react during a zombie apocalypse. It just makes it that much scarier because, y'know, the world *could* face extinction by some bizarre plague sooner or later—or not.

Sin City, story and art by Frank Miller

Did you see the movie *Sin City*? Did you like it? Okay, now read the comic. Frank Miller is, in my opinion, the master of noir comics. Basin City, or "Sin City," is overrun with crime and even has an entire neighborhood (Old Town) dedicated to prostitution. The Basin City police are just as brutal as the criminals, carrying heavy artillery and wearing full body armor. The *Sin City* series is full of "yarns," or different stories, that can be read out of sequence. The whole thing has a very old-school, film-noir quality to it. Miller's illustrations are mostly black and white with little pops of color here and there, most notably in *That Yellow Bastard*. As a matter of fact, I recommend that you start with that book. The old "cop's got one more hour before he's officially off the beat and a retiree, when in walks a dame with a request he can't refuse" takes on a twist when Hartigan gets a call about a kidnapped eleven-year-old girl *he must save*.

Strong Females and Superheroes

Birds of Prey, various writers and illustrators, depending on the issue

Ah, here we are: smart, hot, competent, *female* superheroes. (You may remember this as a 2003 show on the WB.) *Birds of Prey* tells the story of Barbara Gordon (aka Oracle, formerly known as Batgirl), Dinah Lance (Black Canary), and Helena Bertinelli (Huntress). They're sort of like the Deadly Viper Assassination Squad in *Kill Bill*, but fighting for good, not bad. Their characters are handled with skill, conveying strength without getting too far into the superhero clichés. There's lots of "getting over the past" and "moving on with one's life" story lines, and as cheesy as it sounds, that can be sort of inspiring if you're going through a personal crisis of your own. *Birds of Prey* was originally written by Chuck Dixon in 1996 and taken over by Gail Simone in 2003. Start with the Chuck Dixon era if you want a good basis for pursuing the series; it's the trade paperback *Birds of Prey*.

Y: The Last Man, story by Brian K. Vaughan, art by Pia Guerra

You might be torn on this title at first. The basic premise is that a plague has struck the world, killing everyone and everything, even animals, that possesses a Y chromosome—*except*, of course, *one* man and his sidekick monkey. Yup, Yorick is the last man on earth and wants to know exactly why. Jeez. How clichéd can you get? The way that Yorick tosses out, "Calm down, ladies" and "Relax!" as if women are a bunch of hormonal bitches ready to throw down at a moment's notice, also may annoy you. And if we did just happen to be hormonal, "calm down" and "relax" are the exact words that would make us *want* to throw down. You may think that this was created for a bunch of horny teenage boys who are like, "Okay, okay, when do we get to the *good* stuff? Heh heh heh."

So why am I recommending this, aside from the fact that everyone I know seems to love it (and no, not all of them are guys)? Well, it's co-created and penciled by a woman, Pia Guerra. And it's got a sense of humor. I went from being offended to actually laughing. Stick with it! Or start with volume 2. It gives you a nice little summary called "The End of the World As We Know It." It starts to seem as though Yorick is just as stereotypical and bone-headed as all the girl-on-girl situations portrayed in the book (at one point, he actually says to a woman who references science fiction classic *The Man Who Fell To Earth*, "I didn't think pretty girls were into that kind of stuff." So over the top!). Plus, listing the statistics of what the world has lost since the plague (worldwide, 85 percent of all government representatives are dead in *Y: The Last Man*) is sort of a call to arms for the ladies, y'know? I suggest starting with *Y: The Last Man*:

Cycles. It all starts coming together and Yorick's frat-boyisms won't bother you as much.

Black Comedy/Satire

The Boys, story by Garth Ennis, art by Darick Robertson

For some reason, whenever I think about the title of this comic, I get that song "Let's Hear It for the Boy!" from the *Footloose* soundtrack stuck in my head. But this ain't no tale of teenage angst because dancing is banned. Oh no. This is raw. Ladies, be forewarned: There's tons of nudity, sex, violence, etc. The reason why it's funny? Well, the writer, Garth Ennis is behind books like *Hellblazer* and *Preacher*, and has an obvious disdain for superheroes, so if you're down on that genre, you'll enjoy the satire. *The Boys* is actually a parody of the whole superhero genre. The story line follows a team that's been set up within a secret department of the U.S. government to keep superheroes in check. Start reading it with a tongue-in-cheek attitude.

What Have We Learned?

- Comic books aren't just for kids; they're an effective artistic medium.
- That's what your geek has been trying to tell you all along, although you still can't help but hope he gives up the dream of becoming a famous comic book artist.
- As a matter of fact, comic books are sort of like the best of both worlds: movies and novels.
- Comic book store employees really *do* want to help you.
- You still can't touch your geek's collection.

Manga and Anime Geeks

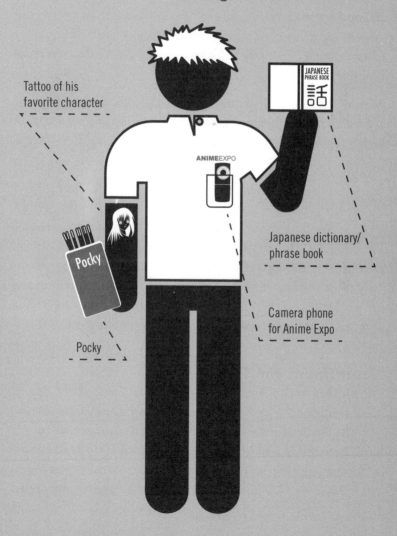

Tattoo of his
favorite character

Japanese dictionary/
phrase book

Camera phone
for Anime Expo

Pocky

Before we even start to look at the wonderful world of teenage ninjas and transforming zodiac animals, there are three important terms you need to know:

Manga (pronunciation varies; often mahn-guh or main-guh; noun): Japanese comic books with artwork and, often, story lines that are distinctly different from their North American counterparts.

Anime (ah-nee-may or an-uh-mey—the hard-core geeks prefer the first pronunciation; noun): This is Japanese animation that's often based on manga.

Otaku (o-tah-ku; noun): This is Japanese slang for obsessed fans, usually of manga and anime (although the term often applies to gaming and science fiction fans, as well). It's derived from a combination of Japanese terms that refer to a way of speaking that is polite and distant and uses formal pronouns—sort of like calling your friend "ma'am." It used to be a derogatory term, but now it's more or less equivalent to "geek" in the United States—if you consider "geek" to mean someone who is obsessed with or an expert in a particular, obscure field.

Super Happy Fun Time!

"Super Happy Fun Time!" is a phrase that came about due to the incongruent way that Japanese is often translated or the way the Japanese themselves use English to market their products. Even if you don't recognize this phrase, you already know what manga, anime and otakus are, even if you think you don't. *Speed Racer*? A U.S. adaptation of a manga and anime called

Mach GoGoGo. Yu-Gi-Oh? A manga that turned into an anime that turned into a franchise, causing a collection frenzy. *Dragon Ball* and *Dragon Ball Z?* Again, a manga that turned into an anime turned into a franchise. Pokémon? Duh. And who hasn't owned at least one thing made by the Sanrio Co., such as Hello Kitty and Badtz Maru?

So manga and anime are more pervasive in our culture than you might have thought at first. What about otakus? Yup. He's sitting in your living room, reading *Berserk.*

He'd have a field day in Japan, if he hasn't visited already. Otaku culture is accepted there, even if it isn't "cool" in and of itself. But otaku "products" are. Manga and anime are used to brand merchandise and to educate children, and they are presented in a mass-oriented way to cause consumer cravings. Manga can be bought everywhere in Japan, from train stations to convenience stores.

An Acquired Taste, Like Sushi

But for some, especially Americans, manga and anime are an acquired taste. The format is truly bizarre and often doesn't make sense in the context of our culture. The women—or should I say girls—in the format are often festishized as teenagers, mostly in some sort of uniform. There is a proliferation of mecha (giant mechanical things), talking animals, people dressed as animals, and, yes, even people having sex with animals. Story lines are twisted and hard to follow, may be downright creepy, or not have a point. Titles are nonsensical (*Strawberry 100%, Boys Be . . .*) yet, to some, awesome in their nonsensical-ness. The style of the artwork is very different from American comics or animation. A lot of times anime has super-cheesy music that might seem overwrought and lame. I'm not trying to scare you off here. The picks I recommend definitely don't err on the side of fetish, and they have a zero creep factor. But you deserve all sides of the story, so when you pick up the wrong manga by mistake, you won't be put off the medium.

Just Like the Mall, There's Something for Everyone

But trust me: There is something, truly *something*, for everyone when it comes to manga and anime. Despite the fact that they can consist of some creepy content, as discussed previously, manga and anime have a slightly more feminine slant than American comics. There are lots of young adult titles that focus on romance with beautiful, androgynous boys, and there are more mature titles that offer, shall we say, a little indecency with their romance? In Japan, manga and anime have a much bigger female following than traditional American comic books. This also holds true right here at home. Why? Maybe because manga and anime characters are often so friggin' cute. They typically have big, expressive eyes, and often seem adorably childlike even when exhibiting very tough attributes. But if this doesn't appeal to you, rest assured that not all manga and anime are like that. There is a high concentration of crime titles with gekiga (illustrations that are much more complex and dark) as well as titles that follow complex and sophisticated story lines.

I'M NOT ALONE, YOU'RE NOT ALONE

Stacey Frost from Birmingham, England, hosts the all-girl podcast *Comic Racks* with partner Iz.

▶▶ "When I started learning Japanese five years ago, I took the opportunity to get my geek on and started to pick up a few mangas, *Bleach* (a "Shônen manga," typically for boys) being my favorite. Fast-forward a couple years, and I meet my lovely boyfriend, Rich. He prides himself on being a nerd and obviously could see my inner nerd screaming to get out. Knowing that I wanted to get into comics, and just getting back into comics himself, he went out and bought the latest Cap issue: Brubaker and Epting's Captain America #15. After that, my inner geek couldn't stop!"

Have you met your Rich yet?

Every Day Can Be Halloween for Cosplayers

"Cosplay" is short for "costume play." Sounds sort of creepy, right? Like "water sports." Ew. But cosplay is actually pretty innocent—well, if you consider a grown man teasing his bleached blonde hair, tying on a headband, and fashioning ninja stars out of cardboard and tinfoil "innocent." Cosplay is mentioned briefly in the comics chapter, but let me explain a little bit more about it here, since it's such an integral part of the otaku community and is super prevalent at all conventions, especially anime and manga conventions. Cosplay is when people get dressed up in costumes that represent their favorite character, whether it's from comics, manga, or anime. Sometimes you

71

even get a random, inexplicable Hamburglar. In Japan, cosplay-ers get together every weekend in the Tokyo neighborhood of Akihabara and . . . perform. I'm talking singing, dancing, and acting. There are even special cafés for otaku called "maid cafés," which capitalize on the maid fetish. Cosplay is tied into lots of RPGs and LARPing (live action role-playing), in which otakus pretend to be the characters they're dressed as.

But look at it this way: Did you dress up last Halloween? What were you? (Please don't tell me "sexy cat/nurse/nun/librarian/etc.") Did you have fun? Mmm hmm, thought so. And when someone walked by you and your friends and yelled an obvious observation while smacking your butt, "Oh my god, it's the three blind mice!" did you then pretend to actually *be* blind and trip him with your cane "by accident"? That's cosplay!

A Brief History

The histories of manga and anime are directly related, since so many anime are live-action animated versions of manga. It's a very complicated history that is tied in to political events both pre- and post-World War II. Some say that most Japanese manga and anime were actually shaped by North American pop culture and U.S. GIs' comic books. Others stress that manga is solely a Japanese form of art that's influenced not by Western culture but by Japanese culture and traditions throughout history. During the post-occupation years (1952 to the 1960s), at a time when Japan was unstable and attempting to rebuild itself, there was an explosion of creativity, producing some of the most famous manga to date.

1902: *Shôjo Kai* (*Girls' World*) was the first notable monthly magazine to contain serialized manga. One can assume that in 1902, most of the stories revolved around pleasing one's husband.

1907: The oldest known clip of anime was a three-second clip of a sailor boy.

1946: Machiko Hasagawa (one of the first well-known female manga artists) creates *Sazae-san*, Japan's longest-running manga strip about the life of housewife Sazae Fuguta.

1950–1969: Two major manga and anime genres are solidified during this time span: shônen (for boys) and shôjo (for girls).

1951: Osamu Tazuka creates *Astro Boy*. Tazuka is considered the "God of Manga" and has been a huge influence on not only most mangakas (manga artists) but also on the entire manga industry. He provided the blueprint and foundation for the medium. He's even been honored with his own museum in his hometown of Takarazuka.

1963: The *Astro Boy* anime series launches.

1969: *Sazae-san* is adapted into an anime series.

1969: The all-women Year 24 group makes its shôjo manga debut. These women were the first to make a major mark on manga, with complex and strong female characters who had their own identities.

1971: Riyoko Ikeda, Year 24 member, creates the popular shôjo manga *Berusaiyu no Bara*.

1975: Haigo Moto, also a Year 24 member, creates *They Were Eleven*, a shôjo manga that challenged traditional Japanese views of women.

1980s: Anime and manga develop a following in the United States, mostly because people are taking the time to translate them. *Akira*, published in 1982, is one of the most famous from this era. Anime dominated the market. Unlike the thick volumes of tankôbon (See "Important Terminology"), animated series were easier to translate.

1986: Viz Communications forms as one of the first U.S. publishers of English-language manga and anime.

1989: CLAMP, another all-female manga group, forms. They start as dôjinshi (sort of like fan fiction; see page 153) creators, but evolve into mainstream manga.

1991: Naoko Takeuchi produces *Sailor Moon* first as a manga, later as an anime. *Sailor Moon* popularizes the concept of sentai, or a team/army of magical girls.

1995: Essential science fiction-ish series *Ghost in the Shell* is published.

1996: TokyoPop, another major U.S. publisher of manga and anime, launches.

1995–1998: *Sailor Moon* is exported to more than twenty-three countries, including the United States.

2002: The first American edition of popular *Shonen Jump* magazine is released. It includes installments of *Yu-Gi-Oh!* and sells almost 300,000 copies.

2004: Americans adapt *Astro Boy* (or *Astroboy* in the states) as a cartoon. Fans are very unhappy with the dub and musical score.

2005: The publishers of *Shônen Jump* introduce *Shôjo Beat*, directed at girls.

Important Terminology

Akiba/Akibahara: This is a neighborhood in Tokyo that is like the mecca for otaku and visiting geeks and nerds. There are cosplay performances in the street and any and every type of item a true otaku could ever want (toys, manga, anime, etc.).

Bishôjo/bishônen: This term refers to a young, pretty (often underage-looking) girl or boy character.

Chibi: deformed characters, usually with heads or limbs that are disproportionate to their bodies

Dôjinshi: This is similar to independently published comics here in the United States, with a couple of big differences. Dôjinshi often utilizes existing characters from popular manga and anime, sometimes parodying them, sometimes creating whole new story lines for them. This is very similar to fan fiction in the United States; the difference is, in Japan dôjinshi is celebrated as an art form and actually sells just as well as traditional manga. Some even say it's revitalized the Japanese manga scene. Artists and publishers tend to look the other way. Copyright attorneys everywhere break into a cold sweat.

Ecchi: art ranging from sexual and fanservice-y (see next page) to partial nudity

Fanservice: In manga and anime, it's the unnecessary inclusion of sexy content. It could be nudity, sex, or just a bishôjo dressed in a maid uniform. It's "servicing" the "fan" and giving him what he wants.

Gekiga: realism, often very dark and bleak realism, in manga and anime art

Hentai: This refers to the pornographic category of manga and anime, and includes extreme fetishes such as bondage, rape, and, er, tentacles. It's not usually referred to in a positive way.

Josei: Manga and anime for older women, it's more explicit and less idealized than shôjo (see below).

Kawaii: the cult of cute

Lolicon: Short for "Lolita complex," it's the idealizing of very young girls in manga and anime and attributing adult qualities to them.

Mangaka: This is the Japanese word for a comics artist; in the United States, the author of a manga is often referred to as the mangaka.

Mecha: basically, giant robots

Moe: This term refers to childlike, submissive, and beyond adorable female characters. It is also used as slang for girls or women who exhibit these qualities.

Seinen: This manga and anime directed at older males often has more violence, nudity, and darker subject matter than shônen.

Shinigami: the manifestation or personification of death; a death god

Shinobi: the ninja, who practices ninjitsu or ninpo

Shôjo/shoujo: This term refers to manga and anime that target girls and women and put more emphasis on plot and character development. Also, there's more focus on love relationships and friendships, as well as magic and fantasy, than in shônen.

Shojo Beat/Shonen Jump: the top two manga mags in the United States

Shônen/shounen: This term refers to manga and anime that target boys. Often you'll see "fighting" anime featuring mecha and characters that possess special super powers. Action is sometimes emphasized over plot.

Tankôbon: A collection of a manga series released in a book-size volume, it's similar to trade paperbacks in U.S. comics.

Yankee: Japanese bad boy or girl

Yaoi: Meaning "boys' love," yaoi (sometimes called Shônen-ai) is marketed mostly toward young women and is very popular in Japan.

Year 24 group: The first group of women to break into manga, it comprised Hagio Moto, Riyoko Ikeda, Yumiko Oshima, Keiko Takemiya, and Ryoko Yamagish.

Yuri: This term means "girls' love" (also called Shôjo-ai).

Special Pointers

1. Manga is read back to front, right to left. You start at what is normally the back cover of the book. Sometimes it's hard to follow the story this way; your eyes aren't used to it. Occasionally, the panels are organized in an odd manner, as well. But publishers like TokyoPop put a "guide" on the last page of the book, which is usually the first page for us American readers.

2. Manga is often very dense. Each tankôbon can have up to 500 pages. If this seems overwhelming, try the anime version of the manga first (even if the manga came first). I did this with *Ghost in the Shell*. You still can be intrigued and inspired to seek more information on it.

3. Always start with the first volume of the tankôbon. Since manga is often complicated, with marked cultural differences in continuity, you may be totally lost if you pick up the second volume first, even if you already know the story line.

4. You should know the following Japanese suffixes so the story makes more sense (they're used mostly for manga):
   -chan: a suffix added to someone's name to denote affection, mostly used with girls
   -kun: same as "chan," but for boys
   -san: a formal way to refer to someone who is equal in social stature to you (the equivalent of Mr. or Mrs.)
   -sama: same as "san," but for someone who holds a higher social position than you

5. Manga and anime genres are more diverse than U.S. comics. In addition to the usual action/adventure, science fiction, and horror, there's romance, comedy, school life, sports, aaaand all the fetishes. So again, when choosing

a manga or anime, think about what your interests are—what kinds of movies you like, what kinds of books you like to read.

Getting to Know Shônen and Shôjo— Beginner Level

For your first foray into manga and anime, I'll break both down into shônen and shôjo. But feel free to read across categories, or just ignore the categories altogether, like a lot of people do.

Most of these recommendations are very accessible, which means you can either pick them up at your local comic book store (be sure to get the first volume tankôbon of each series) or catch episodes on Cartoon Network or the Internet. Otaku will, no doubt, hotly debate me on my recommendations, as everyone has a strong opinion. Some manga and anime fans can seem pretentious, with that attitude of "I was reading/watching this back when no one even knew about it, and all you TV and Cartoon Network fans have made it sooo mainstream, and now I just get everything off the Internet; I don't even bother with that pedestrian stuff—oh, and did I mention I spent a summer abroad in Japan?" I hope that your otaku isn't like this. We all knew about *something* before someone else, and everyone starts somewhere.

Shôjo Manga

Vampire Knight by Matsuri Hino

The Goth in me strikes again. If you were a sucker (get it?) for Anne Rice's *Interview with the Vampire* trilogy in high school, you'll like *Vampire Knight*. Vampire lovers often are classified as totally nerdy. But in Japan, vampire/gothic culture is *huge*—check out the style mag *Fruits* for examples of gothic Lolita style.

But I digress! *Vampire Knight* is the story of Yuki and her duty as guardian at Cross Academy (ha ha again) to protect two separate classes: day students (humans) and night students (vampires). Kanami Kuran helps Yuki with the night class as a guardian, and Zero Kiryu is a guardian for the day class. Forbidden romance, dark secrets, hotly drawn, romantic guys—what more could you ask for except a Kanami in real life?

Fruits Basket by Natsuki Takaya

At first, this manga may seem too simplistic and childish. However, the more you read, the more you'll get caught up in lead character Tohru Honda's enthusiasm and acceptance of all that is different, as well as the inner strength she maintains by thinking of what her dead mother would have wanted her to do in certain situations.

Tohru has found herself homeless, and while exploring the woods she stumbles upon the house of the Sohma family, a family who holds a secret, which is that they turn into animals of the Chinese zodiac whenever a member of the opposite sex hugs them. Tohru begins living with a few of the (very attractive, of course) male Sohmas, promising to keep their secret no matter what.

Fruits Basket may seem cute and funny, but later volumes delve deeper into conflict. Tohru's personality will make you feel so fresh and so clean—as if you, too, could be a Pollyanna. No wonder it's the best-selling shôjo manga title in the United States.

Shôjo Anime

Sailor Moon, based on manga by Naoko Takeuchi

Sailor Moon is considered a maho Shôjo, or a "magical girl" anime. (I know, enough with the terminology already, right? Sorry. These are just things you should know.) It's a huge franchise, and the general concept revolves around a team (or sentai) of magical girls who transform into superheroines to help battle evildoers. There's a heavy dose of mythology, symbols, and fantastical stuff. Don't look for realism here. If this isn't your thing, you should know about it anyway, just because the franchise is so huge and really popularized the concept of the sentai.

Cowboy Bebop, directed by Shinichiro Watanabe and written by Keiko Nobumoto

Cowboy Bebop is an interesting combination of shôjo and shônen. There's action and adventure (in the year 2027, a group of bounty hunters travel through space on their ship, the *Bebop*) mixed with lots of romance. *Cowboy Bebop* is sort of considered anime for people who don't like anime, and is easily accessible. Unlike most anime, it's known for its awesome soundtracks utilizing jazz from the 1950s and 1960s as well as contemporary sounds that are often faux versions of popular Western artists. They have that designer-imposter feeling—you know, "If you like Giorgio, you'll *love* . . ." Don't let the kiddie-sounding name fool you; *Cowboy Bebop* is definitely for grownups, too.

Shônen Manga

Akira by Katsuhiro Otomo

As of the writing of this book, it is rumored that a live-action (aka *movie*) version of *Akira* is in the works, with Leonardo di Caprio as the title character. In 1988, *Akira* was made into an animated film, and played a large part in increasing awareness and interest in anime in the Western world.

It's the year 2019, post-World War III, in neo-Tokyo, and biker gangs rule the streets. There's civil unrest and a corrupt government overseeing a puppet military that attempts to control the violence. Considering that this series began in 1982, it's sort of an interesting prediction, don't you think? Anyway, teenager Tetsuo, a member of a Japanese biker gang, has been subjected to government medical experiments that unleashed his psychic powers. He has these "powers of the universe" at his disposal to search for Akira, a mysterious figure said to be the savior of neo-Tokyo. Classic science fiction themes and intense violence abound. If that doesn't do it for you, just picture Leo as Akira, okay?

Bleach by Tite Kubo

Nominated for several American anime awards, *Bleach* tells the story of Ichigo Kurosaki, a high school student who "sees dead people." Yes, it's very *Sixth Sense* in that Ichigo becomes responsible for helping their souls rest in peace. But! Rukia, a female soul reaper (or shinigami, death god) enters the picture, hunting a Hollow (evil spirit) that has come to Ichigo's town. Rukia is wounded in her battle with the Hollow, and gives her powers to Ichigo, who becomes a rookie soul reaper. Action, action, action! Rukia is saucy and snappy, and you'll love her attitude.

Shônen Anime

Naruto, based on a manga by Masashi Kishimoto

If you have younger siblings, you probably already know about *Naruto.* It's *huge* with the kids, which is why you may have already dismissed it as too young. But if you're committed to learning about anime and manga, it's a must-see from a historical standpoint, in that it's probably the most popular series ever. Naruto is the name of the main character, who starts out as a mischievous orphan in his small village and has dreams of becoming a powerful ninja. And guess what? He does become a powerful ninja! This is kind of the "something for everyone" anime: There's fighting, more blood than you'd imagine, love triangles, family relationships, and tests of friendship.

Ah! My Goddess, based on the manga series *Oh My Goddess!* by Kosuke Fujishima

Remember the classic 1980s movie *Weird Science,* about two geeks who create their perfect woman and bring her to life? This is the same idea but with those weird little twists that only the Japanese can add. Keiichi Morisato is your typical otaku, obsessed with mechanics and anything mechanical and completely unsuccessful with the ladies. One night, Keiichi attempts to call for food delivery, but somehow gets put through to the "goddess hotline" instead. The old cliché "careful what you wish for" applies in Keiichi's case because, of course, he wishes for his perfect girlfriend but instead gets Belldandy, whose completely inappropriate actions get him kicked out of his dorm. *Ah!* It's more fantastical than *Weird Science* because, duh, you can get away with so much more when you use animation. It's cute. It's funny. Otakus love it. Guess why.

Getting to Know Shônen and Shôjo—Moving Beyond Beginner

You've got your Japanese slang down, you called your friend's new haircut "kawaii," and reading right to left, back to front has become way more natural for you, so natural, in fact, that you picked up *US Weekly* and automatically flipped to the last page. You're ready to go beyond the basics.

Shôjo Manga

Banana Fish by Akimi Yoshida

Banana Fish, whose title supposedly is based on a J.D. Salinger short story, is credited with revolutionizing the shôjo genre by including more adult themes. It's actually categorized as josei. When I say "adult themes," I mean sex and violence. (Starting to notice a pattern with manga and anime?) I haven't run across too many shôjo/josei manga that feature lines such as "Know how to use an M-16, pops?"

In 1973, an American soldier goes crazy and starts gunning down his platoon. A fellow comrade, Griffin, injures him, but he's now in a coma, and the only phrase he utters is the mysterious "banana fish." Twelve years later, Griffin's younger brother Ash is a well-respected gang leader on the streets of New York City—that is, until a rash of suicides sweep the city and a dying man crawls into Ash's arms, depositing a vial of mysterious liquid and muttering, "Go to Banana Fish." This is an epic crime drama, and it does feature yaoi as well as drug use. *Banana Fish* is wildly poplar among Japanese teen girls. Is it the yaoi or the insane attractiveness of Ash, who was supposedly modeled after River Phoenix? Perhaps it's the fact that *Banana Fish* is set in NYC, as opposed to the usual manga set either in a fictional land or someplace in Japan. It's sort of funny to see Akimi Yoshida's interpretation of Western street slang.

Kare Kano by Masami Tsuda

The main character is Yukino Miyazawa, a Japanese high school freshman who is a total attention whore and strives to be the best at everything—and always succeeds. Her classmates think she's perfect and are totally jealous of her, but what they don't know is that she's a total poseur. At home, Yukino is spoiled, vain, selfish, and a slob. Enter Soichiro Arima, a hot newcomer who scored higher on the school entrance exam than Yukino did, which drives her up the wall. He steals the spotlight from her and sees through her facade, threatening to topple her position as leader of the class. But guess what? They wind up falling in love! Bet you never would have seen that one coming. No matter. It may be clichéd, some parts may be trite, but then again isn't *Gossip Girl*?

Shôjo Anime

Boys Be . . . , based on a manga by Masahiro Itabashi

Technically, this is considered a shônen series, but I totally disagree. It's sort of like a Japanese anime mishmash of *Pretty in Pink*, *Fast Times at Ridgemont High*, and *The OC*. Oh, and it's from a teenage guy's perspective, which means there's some boob groping and peeks up girls' skirts and verbal dissection of the female body, which is what makes it a shônen series, even though I personally think the story lines lend themselves more to shôjo, which is why I'm putting it here. There's even one character, Makoto, who totally will remind you of Stef in *Pretty in Pink* or Chuck on *Gossip Girl* (hello, *hot*)—you know, cocksure and sleazy. Each episode could stand alone, although you might want to make sure you're up on the characters' personalities by watching episode 1. Usually at least one of the characters has some sort of teenage "epiphany" at the end of the episode, and there's always a cute Zen-like quote to sum up each episode.

The GokuSen, based on a manga by Kozueko Morimoto

Imagine if Meadow Soprano, daughter to mob boss Tony Soprano, had gone on to star in her own series, in which she becomes a schoolteacher at an all-boys school. Her class is out of control, total juvenile delinquents, beyond disrespectful. The naive, happy-go-lucky personality she is assuming to cover up the fact that she is, indeed, the heiress to her mob-boss father's throne isn't really flying. Of course, there's that one student who suspects Meadow is hiding something: When she leaves class, she immediately switches back to her true self, that of a tough mob boss's daughter who constantly spouts "fuggedaboutit."

Now switch "Meadow" with Kumiko Yamaguchi, "mob" with the Oedo Group yakuza clan, and "juvenile delinquents" with yankees, and you've got *The GokuSen*. It's a very short series, which is a real bonus in anime; most are long and complex, and it takes a while to get through them.

Shônen Manga

Death Note, written by Tsugumi Ohba, illustrated by Takeshi Obata

Have you ever been so pissed at someone or something that you could just *kill* them? Like the dude with ten six-packs of beer and ten bags of chips in the grocery express lane, who says, "What? Beer and chips? That's two items!" Or your boss who pulls the whole Bill-Lumbergh-in-*Office-Space* thing: "Yeahhhh, I'm going to need you to go ahead and come in on Sunday." I don't mean literally kill them, of course. But you think it: "God, I could just *kill* them."

Good thing you haven't run across the Death Note, like our antihero Light Yagami. Light, a stereotypical bored, straight-A student, happens upon a notebook dropped by a shinigami, or death god. He soon discovers that any human whose name is written in the book dies. Light vows to use the power of the Death Note to rid the world of criminals and evildoers. But when this starts happening en masse, the police and the public understandably freak out. Mysterious, legendary detective L is put on the heels of this "serial killer," who's been dubbed "Kira," derived from the Japanese word for killer. Is Light really as innocent as he seems? Has he allowed the power and the repercussions of the Death Note to influence his entire life? How would *you* deal with that power? (Dun, dun, DUN! Insert dramatic music here.) Check it out: *Death Note* is wildly popular, heavily addictive, and probably one of the most mainstream mangas out right now.

Battle Royale by Koushun Takami and Masayuki Taguchi (also a live-action movie and a novel, from which the manga was derived)

There's just something about a group of Japanese high school students slaughtering one another willy-nilly that is way creepier than your run-of-the-mill greasy serial killer. In futuristic Japan, there exists a television show called, simply, *The Program*. Every year by lottery, a high school class is chosen to participate in the show. How lucky, right? Quite an honor, wouldn't you think? Hell to the no. The motto of *The Program*? Kill or be killed. Last man (or woman) standing wins. The class is taken to a deserted island, given weapons, and told that if no one dies in the first twenty-four hours, the electronic collars fitted around their necks will explode, killing *everyone*. *Battle Royale* is such a study in characters and their motivations. For example, the "gentle giant" of the class, a slower student named Yoshio Akamatsu makes his first kill because his classmates have always picked on him, and maybe this will show them that he's nothing to be trifled with. It's intense, it's bleak, and I love it.

Shônen Anime

Ghost in the Shell: Stand Alone Complex, based on the manga by Masamune Shirow

Remember way back in the 1990s when the word *cyberpunk* became trendy with the rise of the dot-com era? Alienated, brilliant eighteen-year-old hackers were being hired by the government, sixteen-hole Doc Martens were de rigueur, and people actually thought that *eXistenZ* was a good movie. Well, *Ghost in the Shell* takes the true meaning, and not the trendy one, of cyberpunk to heart. It's the year 2030, and special ops task force Public Security Section 9 is in charge of preventing technology-related violent crimes. These crimes are far too prevalent: You've got your cyberbrain-hacking (in laywoman's terms, a cyberbrain is a self-contained unit for a brain, but it acts just like your real brain), your cyberterrorism, cyber this and cyber that. But even though there's plenty of commentary on technology, at its heart, *Ghost in the Shell* is a police thriller, sort of like *Law & Order* except set in the future with better crime-solving tactics and a really kick-ass female member of Section 9, Motoko Kusanagi. One word of warning, ladies: I found this really *dense*, with tons of plot twists. I tuned in during the middle of the series, and had no clue what was happening. (But it interested me enough to seek out more information on it.) That's why, even though this franchise is pretty well known, it's not listed in our beginner section.

Berserk, based on one of the most successful seinen manga series ever by Kentaro Miura

Super happy fantasy warrior fun time! *Berserk* is sort of what you'd get if *The Lord of the Rings* and *Army of Darkness* had a baby: a very violent, vengeful baby. Main character Guts is recruited as a member of mercenaries The Band of the Hawk, led by warrior Griffith. Guts is an interesting guy, to say the least; he's dark, brooding, with a sword as tall as he is and a prosthetic left hand that disguises a cannon. A hand-cannon! Awesome. Guts is obviously one disturbed guy, and through a series of flashbacks, we learn more about the abuse this man has suffered, which leads him to where he is currently, hunting down the "evil" Griffith. Wha wha what? Isn't/wasn't Griffith his boss, so to speak? Well, you'll just have to watch and find out! A couple of warnings: If graphic violence, even of the animated sort, makes you uncomfortable, this might not be for you. There's nudity (mostly of the male variety) and suggested homosexuality, or yaoi, as well. Don't assume that it's just gratuitous violence, though; one of *Berserk*'s themes is the use of power to obtain certain goals, so I'll let *you* figure out whether that is right or not.

What Have We Learned?

- Manga and anime are the Japanese versions of our comic books and cartoons, but with more violence and nudity.
- There's hard-core sex in some of them, but there also are cute, heartwarming stories about relationships as well as complex crime and science fiction dramas.

- Which is to say, there's something for everyone.
- Cosplay is an important part of otaku culture, so much so that entire cafés have been built around the concept.
- If we act "moe" it may turn our otaku on.

Film and Television Geeks

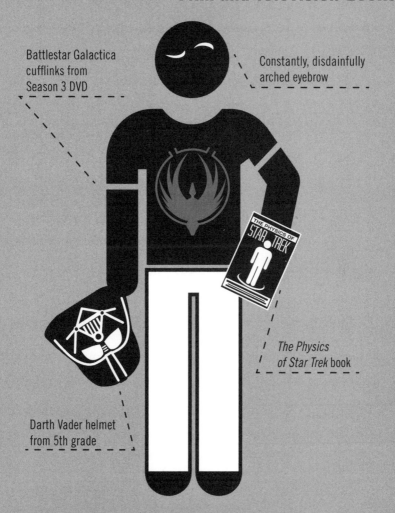

Battlestar Galactica
cufflinks from
Season 3 DVD

Constantly, disdainfully
arched eyebrow

The Physics
of *Star Trek* book

Darth Vader helmet
from 5th grade

What's the difference between someone who likes to watch movies and TV and a true film and television geek? Just to clarify, we're not talking film and television geek of the sort that went to UCLA film school, works in a video store, and talks cinema vérité. We're talking about the film and television geek who is obsessed with nerdy shows! He may not know his deep-focus shot from his reverse shot, but he sure can deconstruct the history of *Buffy the Vampire Slayer*. Here's a little quiz so you can determine if your man's a true film and television geek.

Are You Dating a Film and Television Geek? Quickie Quiz

1. Did your geek have *Star Wars* sheets as a kid? Does he still sleep on them?
2. Do you find yourself dragged to midnight showings of new installments in trilogies so he can be the first one to post his review on his blog (OneRingToRuleUsAll: Trilogy Reviews and Sundries)—a review which may not be positive because "wtf with the lack of continuity?"
3. Did you have a sinking feeling when Triumph the Insult Comic Dog was making fun of nerds in line for *Star Wars: Episode II* because, oh wow, that one in the Obi-Wan Kenobi outfit playing Risk is yours?
4. Has your shared Netflix account mysteriously filled up with *Stargate Atlantis*, *Mystery Science Theater 3000*, *Dune*, and *Aliens*, because they "needed to be revisited"?
5. Did he try to learn Elvish? Klingon? Romulan? Krell?
6. Do you often hear him in insanely circular debates about things like Q vs. The Force or Turbolasers vs. Phasers or Jedis and Rebels vs. Red Shirts?

If you said yes to even one of these questions or if your guy has made a YouTube tribute video of *any* sort, you are dating a film and TV nerd.

The Wide World of a Movie and TV Nerd

It's absolutely crazy to try to encapsulate the world of nerdy film and television, as well as the geeks who live and breathe these shows, in one brief chapter. Well, that's actually been true for all of the chapters, as books can and have been written about each of them. But that's what's been intimidating you, right? The glut of information?

It's especially true with specific beloved films and TV shows because each one is a universe unto itself. There are *Star Wars* fans who run Jedi Council Forums, Trekkies (or Trekkers, as some prefer), Buffyverse obsessives, *Xena: Warrior Princess* RPGers, and *Firefly* Browncoats. But what makes your geek or nerd actually *like* these shows? A lot of them, especially the ones that air on the Sci Fi Channel, seem cheesy. Some of them are watched in an ironic way. Some of them may take you by surprise—*Lost*, a geek show? Yup. So are *Heroes, Terminator: The Sarah Connor Chronicles* (despite the fact that it messes up the timeline to follow, it stars Summer Glau, who played River in the beloved *Firefly* and is "hot"), *Pushing Daisies*, and *30 Rock*. Movies? Well, taking a look at the Comic-Con website to see who's going to be speaking and what film trailers are going to be premiered at this year's con is a pretty good indication of what's flipping your nerd's switch this season.

Okay, So Why Does It Flip His Switch?

Well, you've probably noticed that all of this stuff has something to do with long-form storytelling, space, space travel, time travel, monsters, or special powers. And if it doesn't, it's about people obsessed with that stuff. And if it's not about people obsessed with that stuff, then it's directed by a total film geek like Quentin Tarantino, who is obsessive about detail. If you haven't noticed already, details are very important to your geek. He's hyperaware of them, unlike most people. He's big on continuity, or the lack thereof, which is why some series fall out of favor (witness *Star Trek Enterprise*—Geeks, don't debate me!).

I'M NOT ALONE, YOU'RE NOT ALONE

Artist **Jessicka Addams** says of her husband . . .

▶▶ "He forced me to sit through the entire first season of *Battlestar Galactica*. I actually wound up liking it, but throughout the whole series, whenever someone was faced with a crazy moralistic decision, he'd turn to me and say, "What would you do?" I'd just shrug and say, "I don't know, take a bath?"

Wisdom vs. Innovation

There's an interesting dichotomy between old-school and new-school film and TV geeks, as well. Old-school geeks are usually found in the *Star Trek*, *Star Wars*, *Dr. Who*, and *Lost In Space* category; to them, the concept of futurism is more important than well-developed or likable characters. New-school geeks find the old-school shows and films "quaint," since all that technology is dated now anyway, but still maintain a healthy respect for the classics. New-school geeks would rather watch something with relatable characters and a mix of drama, intrigue, and impossibility. In new-school-geek film and TV, protagonists are faced with decisions your geek will never have to make in his life, such as, should I save the child or let the spaceship blow up?

And let's not forget hero worship, where your geek secretly idolizes the guy who swoops in to save the day. Who hasn't wanted to be adored by millions for his strength, brains, or technological skills?

There is a huge crossover between geeky TV and film and science fiction/fantasy, since most of the geeky TV shows and films *are* science fiction and fantasy. I'm going to focus less on those. You can check them out in the next chapter.

Before we break down the timeline, special pointers, etc.— you know, the building blocks of your film and television nerd's castle, let me just warn you that I'm *not* going to include information on the following:

- Current shows like *Lost* and *Heroes*
- *Buffy the Vampire Slayer*
- Films based on comics
- Anything reality-based (like *MythBusters* or *Beauty and the Geek*)
- 1980s classics you should already know about, such as *The Goonies, Real Genius, Weird Science*, anything John Hughes, but especially *Revenge of the Nerds*

A Brief Timeline

Before we get started—and you can share your newfound wisdom with your guy—I want to make sure you know that this is a timeline of geek and nerd movies and TV shows and geeks and nerds that are *in* movies and TV shows. These are just some of the biggies, and if your indignant geek asks why wasn't such-and-such in here or how could I possibly include *Battlestar Galactica* instead of *Deadwood*, just let him know that he can educate you about whatever it is he thinks I've left out. Okay, here we go:

1966: And so it began. The franchise that will never die (and has way too many series continuations), *Star Trek: The Original Series*, debuts.

1968: Future zombie master George A. Romero directs a small, independent black-and-white film about a zombie holocaust with interesting political subtext called *Night of the Living Dead*. "They're coming to get you, Barbara!" is an oft-quoted line. Have I mentioned how much nerds love zombies?

1977: This is a most holy date for nerds. George Lucas's *Star Wars* is released. May The Force be with you.

1978: *Star Wars* vs. *Battlestar Galactica*! The original *Battlestar Galactica* series airs, and 20th Century Fox sues Universal Studios (*Battlestar Galactica*'s studio) for copyright infringement, claiming that Universal stole ideas from *Star Wars*.

1978: Ten years after *Night of the Living Dead*, Romero's *Dawn of the Dead* premieres, traumatizing yet fascinating young geeks.

1984: Geeks Farmer Ted and Long Duk Dong get the girls in John Hughes' *Sixteen Candles*. A very young John Cusack plays one of Farmer Ted's nerd pals.

1984: The lovable Louis and Gilbert are introduced to college life in *Revenge of the Nerds*.

1985: *Weird Science* is released and officially establishes director John Hughes as king of teenage nerd angst. Oingo Boingo writes the annoying title song.

1992: The *Buffy the Vampire Slayer* film is released. It doesn't do so hot. Creator Joss Whedon goes on to do better.

1993: This is another super holy day for nerds. The *Babylon 5* pilot movie premieres. The TV series debuts in 1994 with a five-season run, but no matter! *Babylon 5* will never die!

1994: *Stargate*, the movie, starts unlocking the secrets of interstellar travel and producing rabid 'Gaters.

1994: The biggest recognized film geek director Quentin Tarantino touches our hearts with his warm tale of friendship, *Pulp Fiction*. His prior film, 1992's *Reservoir Dogs*, was a cult hit, but *Pulp Fiction* does for Tarantino what the iMac does for Apple.

1997: *Stargate SG-1* continues to unlock the secrets of interstellar travel.

1997: Joss Whedon's *Buffy the Vampire Slayer* TV series first airs.

1999: The vastly underrated *Freaks and Geeks* premieres; Judd Apatow overthrows John Hughes as king of teenage nerd angst.

2001: The life of a young Clark Kent, aka Superman, is explored in geek addictive series *Smallville*.

2001: J.J. Abrams' sci-fi/spy TV show *Alias* is first broadcast.

2003: The original *Battlestar Galactica* series re-imagined by the Sci Fi Channel airs.

2004: *Lost*, the series that made me want to clamp my hands over my ears and go, "LA LA LA, *I Can't Hear You!*" when it seemed that every nerd on the planet was talking about it, airs.

2004: Interstellar travel never ends. *Stargate Atlantis*, or *SGA*, first airs as a spinoff of *Stargate SG-1*. Due to scheduling conflicts and the success of *SG-1*, *SGA* is moved to a different "galaxy" so it can run in conjunction with *SG-1*.

2005: Ashton Kutcher's "social experiment" *Beauty and the Geek* first airs. Even geeks and nerds think the geeks on the show are too, well, geeky.

2005: A supernatural phenomenon is investigated by a couple of brothers in the TV series, er, *Supernatural*. Creator Erik Kripke claims Neil Gaiman's *Sandman* as one of his influences. Brothers Sam and Dean Winchester make girl geeks' hearts melt.

2006: Tim Kring delights nerds everywhere with *Heroes*. Character Hiro Nakamura is bona fide nerd.

2007: In *Superbad*, Judd Apatow establishes Fogell (aka McLovin) as the new Farmer Ted but cooler, since nerds are cooler now, you know.

Important Terminology

Wait, what? Are you kidding me? There's no way that I could pick specific terminology from the vast celluloid universe out there. I'll go with key words and phrases and names of different fan factions. You also can learn a couple of curse words in different made-up languages. Listen, there's only so much a girl can do.

Browncoats: fans of Joss Whedon's *Firefly* and *Serenity*

Buffyverse: the entirety of the *Buffy the Vampire Slayer* universe

Computer-generated imagery (CGI): special effects in modern film and TV; replaced stop-motion (you know, like in those Sinbad movies of the 1970s or the myriad 1960s Christmas specials)

Chinese: the language spoken in *Firefly* and *Serenity*, mostly to curse.

Continuity: My god, nerds and geeks are sticklers for continuity. If the timeline of a story is messed up as it segues into its sequel or a different series, it throws the *whole* thing off. Because if terminators were supposed be sent back in time from the year 2029, how come Summer Glau's terminator character in *The Sarah Connor Chronicles* was sent from 2027 yet seems so much more advanced than terminators from 2029? How come? *Tell Me!*

Darth: a title that the Sith Lords, or "bad guys," use in *Star Wars* (What, you thought Vader's first name was "Darth"?)

Director commentary: your film and TV nerd loves it on his DVDs.

Dystopian: Lots of geek TV and films are dystopian in nature, especially futuristic ones where worlds are filled with poverty, misery, and death. It sounds depressing but that's where the hero comes in, and makes things better.

Fanspeak: words, phrases, acronyms, and inside jokes exclusive to fans of a particular film or TV show. Mainly found in science fiction, and of course extends to video games, comic books, etc.

The Force: the powerful "energy" in *Star Wars* that can be used for good or evil

Frak: the "F word" cleaned up for network use in *Battlestar Galatica*

Jedi Knight: Jedi Knights are members of an elite order that observes The Force as a religion, and use The Force to restore and maintain peace within the galaxy.

J.J. Abrams: film and TV producer, writer, director, etc. for *Felicity*, *Alias*, *Lost*, *Cloverfield*, and the soon-to-be-released 2009 version of *Star Trek*

Joss Whedon: writer, director, producer, creator, and on and on for shows like *Buffy the Vampire Slayer* and *Firefly* as well as author to several comic books, including *Fray*, a *Buffy* spinoff; *Astonishing X-Men*; and *Runaways*

Klingons: This is the warrior race in *Star Trek*. Some Trekkers learn the Klingon language at the Klingon Language Institute (KLI). I did not make that up.

Live Long and Prosper: the blessing spoken with the Vulcan hand gesture from *Star Trek*—you know, the hand gesture that involves holding up your hand as if you're going to give a high-five and then parting your fingers between the middle and ring fingers

PetaQ: a very bad way of saying "you piece of crap" in Klingon

Red shirt: This is an inside joke that refers to people in red shirts always getting killed off a series or film. It stems from *Star Trek*, in which the crew members wearing red shirts were always sent out first on missions and usually wound up dead. It's also referenced in *Lost*. Now it's basically used to refer to disposable characters.

"These are not the droids you're looking for": So says Obi-Wan Kenobi while using The Force on storm troopers in *Star Wars: A New Hope*.

Trilogies: Good things come in threes, right? With geeky films they do: Think *The Lord of the Rings*, *Star Wars* (just forget episodes I, II, and III, okay?), *Mad Max*, *Sinbad*, *Back to the Future*, *Spider-Man*, *X-Men* . . .

Whovians: *Doctor Who* fans (see Chapter 7)

Zombie 101: "They're coming to get you, Barbara!"

Lots of geeks and nerds love zombies. Some of them even consider the undead to be social commentary (most commonly exemplified in George Romero's *Night of the Living Dead* and *Dawn of the Dead* and, humorously, in *Shaun of the Dead*), while others just like the complicated effects. There are discussions on exactly where you would take cover during a zombie apocalypse, if you'd rather be a zombie or one of the survivors, and if zombies should move slow or fast. There's even a ZombieCon! There are awesome video games featuring the undead, too (draw your own social commentary). Some oldies but goodies are *House of the Dead* and *Resident Evil*, and some newer ones that are good are *Dead Rising* (zombies in a mall!) and *Left for Dead*.

Some Good Zombie Flicks

Just like your literature teacher always said, you *must* be familiar with the classics! Some of them are dead serious (get it?), some of them are funny, and some of them are funny in their seriousness, but they all should be seen if your geek is a zombie geek.

White Zombie (1932): One of the first zombie classics, it stars Bela Lugosi as "Murder" Legendre.

Night of the Living Dead (1968): Spawned the infamous line, "They're coming to get you, Barbara" and made little girls seems very creepy.

Children Shouldn't Play with Dead Things (1972): The director of this schlocky flick with an unhappy ending, Bob Clark, went on to make *A Christmas Story* and *Porky's*. What a range!

Dawn of the Dead (1978): Intense, bloody, and unrelenting. A true classic.

Zombi 2 (1979): Directed by Italian splatter master Lucio Fulci, this film features the best scene out of any zombie movie ever— a zombie fighting a shark underwater.

Day of the Dead (1985): The third film in Romero's loose zombie trilogy, it's the most depressing.

Re-Animator (1985): Based on the H.P. Lovecraft story "Herbert West: Reanimator," it's best known for a bizarre scene that gives new meaning to the phrase "good head."

Return of the Living Dead (1985): This movie's hilarious and has one of the best soundtracks to a zombie film.

Dead Alive (1992): This gore-fest was directed by Peter Jackson, the same man who brought you *The Lord of the Rings* trilogy.

28 Days Later (2002): One of the best, in my opinion, it completely revolutionized zombie movies and sparked debate on slow vs. fast movement. Oh, and hero Jim is hot.

Shaun of the Dead (2004): Writer/actor Simon Pegg and writer/director Edgar Wright are true geniuses, and this is the best zombie send-up ever.

Getting to Know the Classics—Beginner Level

Here is your introduction to the basic classics. Just to remind you, this chapter is dealing with films and TV shows that are beloved by geeks and not necessarily what film school students would call "art." I'm going to assume that you've seen *Star Wars* and *Star Trek*—how did you start a conversation with your nerd if you haven't? But just in case, here are some pointers.

Star Wars

In the infamous battle of *Star Wars* vs. *Star Trek*, *Star Wars* wins, for me, every time. I do not care that the *Star Trek* phaser is "more accurate" than the *Star Wars* turbolaser. I don't even want to start talking about how much more "realistic" *Star Trek* technology was. The *Star Wars* characters are way more sexy and badass (except those damn Ewoks and the worst character ever, Jar Jar Binks). Princess Leia was my hero when I was a little girl; I loved the way she bossed everyone around.

Not to say that *Star Wars* doesn't have its uber-nerds like Trekkers. The thirtieth anniversary celebration of *A New Hope* at Gen Con *Star Wars* Celebration IV was filled with cosplaying adults and their offspring. And fans are stereotyped as waiting in line weeks or even months in advance for tickets for Episodes I, II, and III . . . because they actually *did*.

Star Wars Films:
- *Episode 1: The Phantom Menace* (1999)
- *Episode II: Attack of the Clones* (2002)
- *Episode III: Revenge of the Sith* (2005)

These are all the "new" *Star Wars* prequel films that give the backstory to the "old" *Star Wars* films. They weren't nearly as good as the "old" *Star Wars*, but that fight in *Episode I* between Darth Maul and Obi-Wan Kenobi and Qui-Gon Jinn has, frankly, been cited by some women I know as "the hottest, most badass scene ever." What about the other, "old" *Star Wars* films? They're listed here:

- *Episode IV: A New Hope* (1977; the original *Star Wars*)
- *Episode V: The Empire Strikes Back* (1980; a lot of fans consider this the best out of the original trilogy)
- *Episode VI: Return of the Jedi* (1983)

I'M NOT ALONE, YOU'RE NOT ALONE

Stars Wars is the "gateway drug" to nerdy film and TV. Take it from **Elisa Collacott,** a librarian who runs the blog *Watching Doctor Who.*

▶▶ "I've been a fan of *Star Wars* since I saw the first film at the age of five, and my favorite movie quote ever comes from *Blade Runner.* I love Buckaroo Banzai, and even have the book. Also, I have two versions of the *Stargate* film, and let's not forget *Serenity.* I have DVDs or old videotapes of *Star Trek: TNG, Buffy, Angel, Stargate SG-1, Red Dwarf, Babylon 5, Firefly,* and, of course, *Torchwood* [a *Doctor Who* spinoff]. If you could only see the 'Big Geeky Notebook,' which holds annotated episode lists of my shows!"

Random Facts That You *Should* Know!

- In 1978, director George Lucas stated that there would be twelve *Star Wars* movies in total. He now says that the plot lines for episodes 10, 11, and 12 have been in his notebooks for more than thirty years.
- From the mouth of the man himself: Darth Sidious is the most powerful Force user in the films. Maybe you can use this piece of knowledge to solve some sort of debate your geek is surely having.

- In *A New Hope*, Han Solo shot first!
- The phrase "do not want" is from a poorly dubbed English-to-Chinese-to-English translation of *Episode III*. Darth Vader's famous "Noooo!" was replaced by "Do Not Want!"
- Jar Jar Binks knocked the Ewoks out of the "most annoying" category. He's just terrible and superfluous.

Star Trek

Okay, I'm gonna be honest with you. I'd be *shocked* if you're actually dating a real Trekkie—unless, of course, you're one yourself, in which case you probably wouldn't even be reading this book. It'd be far too plebian for you. (One note regarding the word "Trekkie": Just as there's a difference between "geeks" and "nerds," there is a difference between "Trekkies" and "Trekkers." A lot of the people whom we call "Trekkies" prefer the term "Trekkers.")

Ever seen the documentary *Trekkies*? No? Watch it. Netflix it, YouTube it, whatever. Trekkies are people (mostly male) who are obsessed not only with *Star Trek* but more specifically with how *Star Trek* basically "predicted the future" of science and technology. As one Trekkie, holding his dog named Computer, put it: "All the stuff that *Star Trek* predicted is actually coming true!"

They do have a point. And a lot of them really are geniuses. But Fanboys are the norm here, and lots of them speak Klingon. "nuqjatlh?" you ask. (That means "huh?" in Klingon, according to my sources.) What's Klingon? It's the made-up language of the Klingon warrior race in *Star Trek*. Start watching the series, and you'll begin to get it. Honestly, though, unless your goal is to completely morph into a Trekker, you don't need to see every single episode or every single series, like *Enterprise,* which is boring and sucks—in my own personal opinion, of course.

Television Series You Should Watch and Know and Love

The Original Series (1966–1969)

The Next Generation (1987–1994)

Deep Space Nine (1993–1999)

Voyager (1995–2001)

Enterprise (2001–2005)

Films:

Star Trek: The Motion Picture (1979)

Star Trek II: The Wrath of Khan (1982)

Star Trek III: The Search for Spock (1984)

Star Trek IV: The Voyage Home (1986)

Star Trek V: The Final Frontier (1989)

Star Trek VI: The Undiscovered Country (1991)

Star Trek: Generations (1994)

Star Trek: First Contact (1996)

Star Trek: Insurrection (1998)

Star Trek: Nemesis (2002)

Honestly? If you ask a *Star Trek* geek, they'll probably tell you to just watch *The Wrath of Khan*, which is the best one and known for the infamous space worms and cry of, "Khaaaaaan!". Oh, and *The Search for Spock* isn't that bad, either.

Random Facts You *Should* Know!

- Spock was half-human, half-Vulcan, and Dr. McCoy always held it over his head. What a jerk! TV honchos, however, were a bit concerned with his "satanic" appearance.

- Pregnant pauses and overacting are what made William Shatner's Captain Kirk so campy and good. Captain Jean-Luc Picard stepped into the Kirk role for *Star Trek: The Next Generation*, and replaces Kirk's histrionics with tea drinking.

- When the original *Star Trek* series was canceled after only two seasons, creator Gene Roddenberry organized a fan letter-writing campaign to bring it back. It worked.

- The famous flip-open communicator design has been copied by many cell phone companies, most notably Motorola. Trekkers are totally right in this case; *Star Trek* predicted the future. In the show, the communicator seemed to exist only as a means of stranding characters by not functioning, being out of range, or getting lost. Just like cell phones today.

- Spurred by yet another letter-writing campaign by fans, NASA named the first space shuttle *Enterprise* after the *Star Trek* starship *Enterprise*.

Television

These are two great series that were on TV but, sadly, have been canceled. Never fear! You can get them on DVD.

Firefly (2002)

I didn't think I would love *Firefly*, but after the BF put the *Firefly* movie *Serenity* in our Netflix queue, I thought I'd check out the series and see what all the fuss was about. At first, it seemed so cheesy. A space-age Western? But halfway through the pilot, I fell in love. Was it the fact that Captain Malcolm "Mal" Reynolds reminded me of Han Solo or that Jayne wielded a huge, er, gun with talent and ease? Maybe.

Joss Whedon, genius that he is, created *Firefly* and, sadly, Fox canceled the series after only eleven of the fourteen episodes had been aired out of sequence. But when *Firefly* was released on DVD, sales shot through the roof, and there were massive fan support campaigns.

The series is set in 2517, after a civil war fought between the Browncoats and the Alliance, who want to govern the entire universe. It follows the travels of nine people aboard *Serenity*, a renegade scavenger ship that takes on odd, dangerous, and often illegal jobs. There's an interesting moral fabric here; situations aren't black and white like they are in most TV shows. There are no sanctimonious epiphanies about how the law is always right, and the line between the "good guys" and the "bad guys" is sometimes blurred. It is really, truly, like a space-age Western soap opera—but without the bad acting and overwrought emotions. As a matter of fact, Captain Mal is so tough and barely shows any emotion whatsoever. When he eventually does, you're all, "Yea! I knew Mal had it in him!" and you can't help smiling.

Hercules: The Legendary Journeys (1994–1999)

There aren't a lot of TV shows that are pure fantasy, but Sam Raimi's re-imagining of the myth of Hercules sure is one of them. And when I say re-imagining, I mean completely different except for the characters. And even then, that's a stretch.

Setting the film in a non-specific time period that could be referred to only as "The Past" or "A Very Long Time Ago," Raimi (also known for his work on the *Evil Dead* Bruce Campbell trilogy and the *Spider-Man* trilogy) takes liberties with Greek mythology and the country of Greece as a whole. But no matter! We have a tanned, buff hero (who may not be your cup of tea, as you are fond of geeks and nerds) traveling around the land with his best friend, Iolaus, saving villagers from gods and monsters alike. *Hercules* has a couple of elements crucial to why your geek likes shows like this: hero worship and a big dose of irony. Familiar centaurs and Cyclops as well as completely made up, fantastical monsters? Check. Comedic sidekick? Check. Scantily clad women, lest all that testosterone become overpowering? Check. Another series spinoff (*Xena: Warrior Princess*)? Check. It's Geek TV 101, ladies.

Getting to Know the Classics—Moving Beyond Beginner

Maybe you skipped to this part because you already have the basics down. Good for you! You'll have to check out Chapter 7 for additional geek film and TV suggestions. But for now, let's do a little more brushing up on some essential geek film and TV obsessions.

Film

Am I cheating by lumping lots of films by a single director into one category? It's up to you to decide!

Kevin Smith Movies

Face it: Kevin Smith is a total film and comic geek. He wrote the first eight issues of the Marvel Knights series *Daredevil* (made into a film starring Ben Affleck). He sold his comic collection to fund his movie *Clerks* (then bought it back with the profits). He owns a comic book store called Jay and Silent Bob's Secret Stash. He inserts ultra-nerdy debates into his films, such as the one in *Mallrats* that revolved around kryptonite condoms and whether or not Lois Lane could carry Superman's baby.

All in all, he has created an entire world with his films that cross-reference characters and incidents, something that film geeks are big on. They say things like:

"If you haven't at least seen *Mallrats, Chasing Amy, Clerks*, and *Dogma*, then there's no way you're going to get the humor in *Jay and Silent Bob Strike Back*. I mean, it's only made for a small percentage of the population, anyway—his *true fans*."

So, if *you're* new to this whole Kevin Smith thing, watch *Clerks*, which is a day in the lives of two New Jersey store clerks. It's funnier than it sounds, really, especially if you've ever worked a mind-numbing retail job where you checked the clock every five minutes: "What the . . .? It was just two o'clock *a half an hour ago!*"

Quentin Tarantino

Okay, I'm cheating again by including a director instead of a specific movie, but Tarantino is the nerdiest, geekiest film freak around—right down to the crazy social awkwardness. He blatantly and proudly flaunts obscure influences, like his homage to martial arts classics *Flying Guillotine* and *Master of the Flying Guillotine* in the *Kill Bill* movies (for example, the martial arts master in *Kill Bill Vol. 2* was named Pai Mei; the star of *Flying Guillotine*, Pai Wei). His films are thick with references and inside jokes, which film geeks *just love*. He often inserts himself into his own story line—hello, total fan fiction habit. His films often contain the completely improbable mixed with reality.

Several years ago, there were even whispers from Tarantino himself about an anime prequel to *Kill Bill*. It still hasn't happened, but who knows?

Television

Here are some serious cult classics! The best way to enjoy them is to get them on DVD and veg out for hours on end.

Freaks and Geeks

The name says it all, no? The series revolves around the everyday lives of brother and sister Sam and Lindsay Weir, and captures all of the awkwardness and self-consciousness of what it's like to be not-so-popular in high school—like when Sam finally gets a slow dance to Styx's "Come Sail Away," and that tempo change in the middle, when it speeds up, throws him totally off his game. Because, really, what do you *do* in a situation like that? Anyway! *Freaks and Geeks* was created by none other than Judd Apatow, the king of 2007 with movies *The 40-Year-Old Virgin, Superbad*, and *Knocked Up*. You'll also see a lot of familiar faces who got their start in *Freaks and Geeks*—Seth Rogen and James Franco, for example—and whom Apatow continues to cast in his films.

Mystery Science Theater 3000

How people call themselves film and TV geeks without liking *Mystery Science Theater 3000* is beyond me. It combines the best of all geeky worlds: robots, space travel, and snarky comments directed at cheesy movies. Joel Robinson (played by standup comedian and toy designer Joel Hodgson) is a janitor at the top-secret Gizmonic Institute (he's replaced by Mike Nelson in later seasons). He's been isolated on the spaceship *Satellite of Love* by two evil scientists, Dr. Clayton Forrester and Dr. Lawrence Erhardt. Their plan? To force Joel to watch bad movie after bad movie so they can study the effects this has on his psyche. Joel has built himself some robots—Gypsy, Tom Servo, Crow, and the camera robot, Cambot—to keep him company on the ship. Tom Servo and Crow join Joel as he watches the bad movies in the "mystery science theater" on board the ship, and they join in the skewering of movies such as *Godzilla vs. The Sea Monster* and *Master Ninja I*. Don't you and your geek do things like this? How could this not be the most hilarious, awesome thing in the world?

What Have We Learned?

- There are common threads running through your geek's favorite films and TV shows: complicated story lines, time travel, space travel, talking about time or space travel, hero worship, conflict, and the creation of entire worlds.
- His love for certain shows and movies is deeply ingrained in childhood, much like your love for *KISS Meets the Phantom of the Park*. Oh wait, is that just me?
- You probably already like some of the shows he watches, and know that . . .
- . . . geeks and nerds have great senses of humor . . .
- . . . except when it comes to *Star Wars* vs. *Star Trek*.

Sports Geeks

Team hat

Team t-shirt

Stats sheet

STATS

FANTASY LEAGUE

Fantasy League CD-ROM

Wait, what? Geeks and nerds and sports? Oh yes. Don't be fooled by their other intellectual pastimes. Don't be fooled by their reed-thin builds. Don't be fooled by the fact that when you tossed him an apple, he immediately shielded his face. There are lots of geeks and nerds who are sports geeks and nerds.

My Background in Sports (Ha)

I was never a sports fan. Don't get me wrong: I appreciate sports, and I was even a gymnast for ten years. But I grew up in a football household. My PhD-holding father was not a total sports nut; he didn't yell at the TV or get angry when his team lost a game. But he had played football in high school and college and enjoyed watching it. I always thought football was bo-ring! Thanksgiving and Christmas days were the worst because I was expected to spend time with the relatives I hadn't seen in a long time while those relatives all watched football. I honestly just wanted to go in my room and read a book.

When I started dating my now-boyfriend, I knew he liked to watch sports every once in a while: the game on Sundays with the boys, maybe baseball during the week, a little basketball here and there (and, yes, this is the same boyfriend who loves to play video games, has a fairly good knowledge of his superheroes, and repaired computers for his college's computer lab). Not my thing, okay, but I could put up with it. He never indicated that he was much more invested in certain sports and teams (football and baseball, Chicago Bears and Cubs respectively) than I thought, maybe as a result of all my derogatory, "God, that is so jock-ish!" exclamations after observing any boorish behavior.

So imagine my surprise when the Chicago Bears lost a major, major game several years back. The BF went into deep, immediate depression and was inconsolable. I made the cardinal mistake of chirping, "What's wrong? It's only a game! They'll do better next year, right?"

Pointer Number One: *Never* say "it's only/just a game." The BF barely spoke to me for a week.

Ever Participated in the "Cool Down" Walk?

You'd think that after learning that lesson the hard way, I'd have had a turning point or epiphany, but oh no. I didn't get over that resistance hump and say, "By golly, I should just start watching the games with him so I can understand why he's so invested in them!" It actually *increased* my hostility toward sports. Sports turned the BF into a growling, grouchy McGroucherson when his team lost. Many walks were taken "to cool down." When his team won, it was endless rehashing thanks to ESPN's *SportsCenter*. He referred to his teams in the most unusual of terms (in my opinion). It wasn't, "They got a touchdown!" It was, "*We* got a touchdown!" Which prompted me to snort, "What, you're on the team now?"

Pointer Number Two: *Never* question his use of the word "we" when referring to his team.

So I retreated elsewhere when he watched games at home. Would this sports stuff *never* end? First it was football season. Then, just when I thought it was all over for a couple of months,

I'm informed that basketball season has been overlapping with football season, so now it's time to watch basketball. Okay, fine, but there has to be a break somewhere, right? No! Next, there's baseball spring training. Then baseball season! Sports. Never. Ends. It's the great American pastime, y'all.

Get in the Game Yourself

There are tons of women who like sports. I have girlfriends who will watch for many different reasons, from "I think their asses look cute" to "I really like the game; it gets the adrenaline going." My mom is a huge Florida Gators football fan, in fact, even more so than my dad. She'll go to games with her best friend, who likes the Tallahassee Seminoles, the rival team. She wears the shirts. I buy her the accessories for Christmas (Gator four-piece barbecue set, anyone?) She, like the BF, also gets very disappointed when the Gators do not win an important game. I guess I didn't get that gene.

Begrudging Attempts at Compromise

But I've been trying. As much as I prided myself on my dislike of sports as some sort of *badge* that I was more intellectual or something, I kind of felt left out. The BF would go to bars on Sunday afternoons to watch the games with tons of Bears fans and have constant conversations with other sports-lovers about the status of their teams.

And here I was, ordering nachos and going, "What's a touchback?"

"Shhhh." I got the hand wave.

So how did I change this? Well, I haven't yet. But I'm trying. And I find that I enjoy sports more and more; for me, there's a sense of inclusion and identity. This may be why your geek or nerd likes sports, too. Like a multiplayer video game, sports offer a way to bond with fellow guys over something that's a bit more socially acceptable than sitting in a dark room hunched over a PC. They always have something to talk about, and there are statistics, numbers, and tons of rules to learn. And we all know how our geeks love those things. They may even have a secret desire to participate, which is totally okay. I'd rather the BF simply watch sports than turn into a beefy jock who starts to lose brain cells because he's been tackled by the boys too much.

Meet Christina, a Fledgling Sports GF

Christina, a self-professed crossword puzzle and book nerd, took to her boyfriend Matt's sports interest a bit better than I did. Now, let's keep in mind that Matt is also a self-proclaimed nerd. He went to band camp and still searches out marching band competitions on TV. But his sport of choice? NASCAR. As in the National Association for Stock Car Auto Racing. He actually enjoys watching cars go around and around a track. It was ingrained in him since childhood, since his father works for Goodyear and happens to be a racing fan. Matt and his friends go to two races each year, and Christina decided that it was time she try it, too. After all, as she put it, "If Matt liked it, it couldn't be that bad!"

Her first race was the Brickyard 400 at the Indianapolis Motor Speedway in July 2006. She and Matt were meeting up with friends from all over the country to camp out on the grounds (this is very big in NASCAR), and had bought some neat new tent that you throw up in the air to open. Before they got there, her excitement was mostly based on the tent.

But all that changed. She got caught up in the moment, in the novelty, and started to, dare I say, enjoy herself immensely.

I'M NOT ALONE, YOU'RE NOT ALONE

Christina Guerin, a NASCAR guy's girlfriend, describes her first NASCAR event.

▶▶ "The thing I liked most about it was the feeling of 'no rules.' You could wear whatever you wanted, do what you wanted, or not do anything at all. No one was judging anyone else; everyone was just there to relax and have fun. It spoke to the rebel in me! I could be myself, however I felt at the moment. I was walking around in a bikini top, shorts, and trucker cap for god's sake, drinking beer, walking around in the sun with a bunch of NASCAR fans. . . . In New York, I wouldn't be caught dead in a trucker cap, but here, no rules. It made Matt so happy and proud, so I wore that damn hat all weekend.

Compromise, Ladies. Compromise.

Since sports go back to prehistoric days, when men wearing bear skins lunged at one another with sticks, it's way too hard to cover "the history" of sports in this one section. So instead, I'll summarize the terminology you need to know. Honestly, if you just throw around some of these words ("Hmm, looks like a touchback; good for the Bears!"), you'll sound as if you know what you're talking about. You don't need to know much about the past to start enjoying sports today. Sure, there are monumental, historical moments in each sport, but to start spelling those out would take a million pages.

One more thing before we continue: If we're truly talking sports geeks and nerds here, we cannot gloss over fantasy sports, which involve your geek's pretending that he is a "team owner" and building a team that competes against other fantasy owners' teams. It's all based on statistics, otherwise known as *numbers*—and we know that geeks love numbers. There are managers of the fantasy team who help compile the statistics, there are league commissioners who total the statistics, and there are even computer programs that process the statistics for the best odds. This is a geek's dream come true. Just about every sport has a fantasy league. I've seen a football one: scrawny guys who are total computer nerds sitting around going, "Any sleeper RBs I should look out for? Should I do this trade or hold out for something better?" It's almost more about the game (your geek might say "the art of") of compiling his team and trading players than it is about the actual *game* itself. And lest you think this is some dark backroom stuff, there are online leagues organized by Yahoo!, ESPN, and CBS.

Special Pointers

1. Feel free to ask your geek all the questions you want—just not during the game. He will flat out ignore you, and that will piss you off because how dare he and it's just a game, and maybe you'll fume, and then later on when he says, "Hey, did you see where I put my wallet?" you'll snap, "Why does everything revolve around sports?!"

2. Try to start identifying with a team. That will give you a more personal connection to the sport of your geek's choice. For example, I started to identify with the University of Florida Gators' football team because I grew up in Gainesville, where the school is located. I began to feel that every victory the team made was a victory for my tiny town, forgetting, of course, how much I hated that tiny town when I was growing up there. No matter! Pick a team. Like their colors? Great. Think the captain is hot? Even better. Everyone else seems to like them? Hey, why not?

3. Ease into it by watching a bit of each game—maybe the first inning or quarter—with your geek. Or watch it with your girls first if they like sports. They won't mind when you interrupt the game to say, "Why'd he do that?" or respond with, "Because he just did!" But keep in mind that a lot of sports rules are not logical and do not make sense.

4. If your geek is the kind who gets sad/depressed/angry when a team loses, go with it. Don't try to cheer him up unless you know exactly the right thing to do. For the BF, it's usually buying a new video game or drinking lots of beer—in silence, of course. And just let him vent. You may not understand why he's asking you, "What happened? Why'd they do that? I can't believe it; can you believe it?" You're thinking, Hey, I didn't even watch the damn game. Just nod and frown; that always seems to work.

5. Don't make him feel stupid for liking sports. It may alarm you that he wants to hang a Chicago Cubs pennant on your bedroom wall. You may think that his decorating taste is lacking, and what are we, a frat house? Just gently

suggest another area where it would look better. Like the closet. Kidding! Don't do that.

Sports Specifics by Type of Game

Since this chapter is an anomaly to begin with, I'm going to dispense with the "important terminology" and a brief timeline. In each section, I'll define sports-specific terms that will be in bold, and, if necessary, you'll get some dates, too—of the number kind, not the geek kind. Although, you never know!

Getting to Know the Games—Beginner Level

First, let's examine what sports are kind of easy to get into; these also are the ones that probably consume your sports geek's waking hours during season. I'm going to make things very simple, and just keep in mind that there is obviously way more to each sport than I can spell out here. Once you're sucked in, you'll surely want to learn more.

Football

Ever heard of the term *football widow*? Right. I forgot; you're living it. Let's get started so you can start enjoying what feels like an endless season.

Each game starts with a **kickoff**. Well, actually it starts with a coin toss to decide who gets the kickoff. The teams start at opposite ends of the field and wait for the ball to be kicked. The team that's supposed to be **receiving** the ball can do one of three things: catch it and try to get it to the other end of the field; **signal** the referee (by waving hands in the air) for a "**fair catch" in order to stop the play where the ball was caught; or signal a **touchback**. A touchback is when the kicked ball lands in the receiving team's **end zone** and the receiver places a knee on the ground (known as "**taking a knee**"); the ball automatically will be placed at the receiving team's twenty-yard line. The receiving team isn't allowed to advance the ball or run the ball down the field after a fair catch or a touchback has been called.

Now, end zone. That's just a football way of saying the big painted area with the goalpost where touchdowns are scored. You do know that each team has to run the ball into the opposite team's end zone to score a touchdown, right? The team that has the ball is referred to as the **offense**, and the team that is protecting its end zone is called the **defense**. You'll also hear terms such as **offensive line**. No, this isn't when some guy at a bar is all, "Hey, baby, are those space pants you're wearing?" The offensive line's job is to protect the quarterback so he can run the ball or throw the ball.

The **quarterback** is the guy on the team who calls the plays, the leader, so to speak. The **coach** sets the plays. The **center** is the guy who throws the ball between his legs so the quarterback can catch it. On either side of the center, there are **guards**. They're, um, guarding him. On either side of the guards are **tackles**. They, er, tackle.

What, there's more? Yes, more players. Hang on, it's almost over. And it wasn't really that painful, was it? Okay, so on either side of the tackles there are one or two **tight ends** (insert hot-ass joke here). There also are **running backs**, whose job it is to run the ball. See how easy this is? And we can't forget the **wide receivers**. They run down the field toward the end zone and catch the ball when the quarterback throws it to them. There are also the defensive players like linebackers, safeties, and strong safeties—but all of these are the main guys you should worry about.

The offensive team has four tries to move the ball ten yards down the field for a first **down**. Downs are all of the attempts that the offense makes to get the ball to the end zone. When the offense runs out of downs and hasn't scored a touchdown, it needs to hand the ball over to the defense (sometimes not without a fight), and the offense and defense switch.

How Long Will It Last?

There are four **quarters**, or parts, of the game. Each quarter is supposedly fifteen minutes, but we all know that's a joke. With time-outs and calling plays and contesting plays and all the other football dramas that go on, an hour game usually lasts about three hours—or longer with overtime. And you *do* know that a game goes into overtime when the teams are tied, right? Right?

No, Really, How Long Will It Last?

The National Football League (NFL) season consists of a preseason (August), regular season (September through December), and postseason (January through February, or whenever the Super Bowl is).

Scoring

Touchdown: 6 points

Extra-point conversion: 1 point (for lining up and kicking the ball through the goalposts)

Two-point conversion: 2 points (for lining up at the two-yard line after scoring a touchdown in order to run the ball into the defense's end zone again)

Field goal: 3 points (occurs when a team has a fourth down and doesn't think it'll make a touchdown but *does* think it's close enough to kick the ball through the goalposts)

Safety: 2 points (when a guy gets tackled holding the ball in his own end zone—oopsie)

Have I lost you yet? Okay, take a break, go get some milk, and maybe take a little nap or something. But if you're really dedicated and tough, read on!

Basketball

In 1891, James Naismith of Springfield College in Massachusetts invented an indoor sport for students to play when it got cold outside. Basketball was originally played with peach baskets instead of hoops. The goal was—and still is—to score more points than the other team by getting the ball through the other team's basket or net.

The game begins with a **tip-off**. The ball is thrown up in the air, and one player from each team attempts to tap it to another player on his or her team. Whoever takes possession of the ball becomes the offense, same as in football.

So now, the offense has to get the ball into the other team's net by dribbling it down the court. The player with the ball may **drive**, or cut toward, the basket to attempt a **lay-up**, or easy one-handed shot that bounces off the **backboard** and into the net. He can always pass the ball to another player, or he may do something called a **jump shot**, where he jumps in the air and tries to make a basket. Or, he may **dunk** the ball, meaning he jumps up and slams it into the net.

This is assuming, of course, that he hasn't been **traveling**, which is going two or more steps without dribbling the ball, which results in a **turnover**, meaning the other team gets the ball; or that the ball hasn't been **stolen** from him, which players on the opposite team can do; or that the defensive team hasn't been executing **press** (full court or half court), which is when they guard offensive players really closely so that they make mistakes.

Even though the game looks fairly simple, there's a lot of crap involved with basketball, such as the possibility of having a personal or technical **foul** called. I guess the game was *too* simple, which is why all the rules were invented. When the offense has the ball, defensive players are totally on their jock, guarding them, trying either to steal the ball or prevent them from throwing it to other offensive players. In **man-to-man defense**, each player guards one player of the offense. In **zone defense**, players guard specific areas of the court, instead of just one player.

How Long Will It Last?

In the National Basketball Association (NBA), there are four twelve-minute periods. There's also a fifteen-minute halftime between the second and third periods. But again, you've got overtimes, you've got fouls, you've got free throws, so you're looking at a three-hour commitment, easy.

No, Really, How Long Will It Last?

Just like football, you've got your pre-season (October-ish), regular season (November through the end of April), and post-season/playoffs (May through June).

Scoring

Free throw: 1 point (for a shot made from the **free-throw line**, a line that you'll definitely see, by a player who's not being guarded)

Field goal: 2 points (for a shot that goes into the basket from within the **three-point line**; the most common way of scoring)

Three-pointer: 3 points (for a shot that is made from outside the three-point line)

Baseball

Baseball started as a version of an English game called rounders. Alexander Cartwright published the first official set of rules in 1845. In my opinion, baseball's a little bit easier to get into than football or basketball. Some may disagree and say it's too boring, that there's not enough physical action, but you be the judge. All I know is that ballpark food is delicious, and I like doing the wave.

The game starts with the visiting team batting in the first half of the inning, called the **top of the inning**. The home team bats at the **bottom of the inning**. Every time a player is **at bat**, which means he's up for batting, he tries to hit the ball so he can then score a **run** by circling all the **bases**. When he's at bat, he wants to avoid getting **strikes**, which occur when he misses the ball or doesn't swing at a good pitch. Three strikes equal an **out**. Come on, tell me you knew that.

There are other ways of getting a player out of the game. There's the **force-out**, in which the defense throws the ball to first base before the offense has time to get there. A **tag-out** is when a player is tagged with the ball when he's not standing on a base. A **fly-out** is when the ball is caught by the defense before it touches the ground. Get two people out at once (usually via a force-out followed by the first baseman's throwing the ball to second base), and it's called a **double play**. Or, if an offensive player isn't being careful enough and starts heading to the next base when the pitcher has already started his pitch, he can get nailed on a **lead-off**.

But the player has tons of opportunities to score via different types of hitting and running. He could hit a **fly ball**, which is a high, arching ball; a **ground ball**, which means the ball's low to the ground (players usually don't score this way, actually); or a **ground-rule double**, which is when the ball bounces in fair territory and goes up and over the fence of the field—the batter gets to go to second base automatically, and any other players on the bases get to move forward two bases. There's also the **line drive**, when the ball is hit so that it travels in a line almost parallel to the ground.

But what are all those players doing way out in the field, you ask? Those are the **outfielders**—more specifically, the left, right, and center outfielders. Closer to the pitcher's mound you've got the **infielders**, or the usual suspects: first, second, and third **basemen**; a **pitcher**; a **catcher**; and a **shortstop**, the guy standing between second and third bases.

Baseball is easy to understand. It has its rules, but they're fairly simple: For instance, only one person can be on a base at a time, and a **foul ball** is a ball hit outside the **foul lines**, which you easily can see (unlike the first downs and stuff in football). Also, since it's "the great American pastime," you can gorge yourself on the aforementioned hot dogs, peanuts, nachos, and beer, all in the name of patriotism. And did I mention that the players look cute in their uniforms?

How Long Will It Last?

There are nine innings, each of which lasts until the hitting team has gotten three outs. You're looking at about three hours, without overtime.

No, Really, How Long Will It Last?

With Major League Baseball (MLB), spring training starts in March, the regular season runs from about April through October, and then playoffs start. The season is over after the World Series.

Scoring

The scoring system couldn't be simpler: Each player who circles the bases and scores a run earns one point for his team.

But there's also this thing that uber-baseball nerds do called "keeping score." They have their own personal scorecards, with different kinds of information such as batter performance (for things like at bats, runs, hits, and **errors**), inning totals, and pitcher performance. Once your nerd has all this info, he can calculate all kinds of fun statistics such as **batting averages** (the total number of times the ball was hit) and stuff. There also are offensive statistics, defensive statistics, pitching statistics, and team statistics.

Getting to Know the Game—Moving Beyond Beginner

Okay! Do you have your team picked out yet? Is your sports geek furiously watching drafts and preseason games and all that, and you're finding you actually have the desire to watch, too? Looking forward to the corner bar's chicken wings? Congratulations! Let's check out some more sports that go beyond the all-American trio discussed above.

NASCAR

"NASCAR" stands for the National Association for Stock Car Auto Racing. There are lots of different versions of car racing, such as Formula One single-set racing (what Sacha Baron Cohen's character did in *Talladega Nights: The Ballad of Ricky Bobby*). Europe's version of NASCAR is Tour Car Racing.

But we're talking about NASCAR, and NASCAR only. What do you think of when you think of NASCAR? Rednecks? Beer drinkin' good ol' boys? Well, yeah, those are some NASCAR fans. But there also are fans like Matt and Christina, whom we heard from in the beginning of the chapter. And there are fans like my parents, who actually travel in their deluxe RV to camp out at different races in the Southeast. And they drink margaritas.

Car racing has been around since the late 1800s, and it started mainly as a way to test cars' performance. The first race in the United States was in 1895. Currently, the two biggest NASCAR races are the **Daytona 500** (one of the most-watched sporting events in the United States and the race that kicks off the NASCAR season) and the **Brickyard 400**.

What's the Point?

Now, I don't really need to tell you the point of car racing, because it's so obvious—you race around a track and the guy who comes in first at the end of the race wins. But what is all that flag waving you see? Well, you know that the **checkered flag** signals the end of the race. Other important flags are the **green flag**, which means the race has started or restarted after a **full caution** or a stop, and the **red flag**, which means the race has stopped. When there's one lap to go, the **white flag** is waved. The **yellow flag** means caution. And the **black flag**? That means someone's in *trouble*!

If a driver gets the black flag, he has to report to the **pit** to get scolded. The pit's the big area in the middle of the track where cars get fueled up, repairs, mechanical adjustments, and even new tires. The tires are obviously insanely important to the driver's car. Sometimes you'll see cars weaving back and forth at the start of a race, during the **warm-up laps**, and that's to warm up the tires and make sure any debris is off. Tiny adjustments to **air pressure** totally can affect the way a car drives. But just in case something goes wrong, a driver is protected by his **roll cage**, or specially constructed frame. You don't want to lose too much time in the race, so a pit stop to change four tires and get fuel can be as fast as *sixteen seconds*. For real.

A fundamental to enjoying your race is to make sure to pick a driver! Whether he's your NASCAR geek's choice or you like his uniform, his car, or the sponsor of his car (there are tons of sponsors in NASCAR, and they advertise on the exteriors of the cars), picking a driver gives you a reason to yell, "Go! Go! Go!"

I'M NOT ALONE, YOU'RE NOT ALONE

Here's another story from **Christina** about her first Brickyard 400.

▶▶ "A live race is a completely different experience. My favorite part was getting the headphones and scanner so you could listen to the TV and radio broadcasts and even get onto the drivers' frequencies and listen to them talking to their crews. Speaking of the crews, I love the uniforms. I guess that's because I'm a designer. And the cars are so much cooler and the colors so much more intense in real life. It was loud, with the engines roaring to life to head toward the start/finish line. The camaraderie of cheering your favorite driver felt good. I had never been a big sports fan, so that was all new to me. After that, I gladly watched races and came to know the drivers on my own. Before the Brickyard 400, it was done out of love for my man. But it's grown into a genuine interest of mine. It's really fun to have this common interest with my boyfriend, one more thing that we can talk about and do together."

How Long Will It Last?
Brace yourself. The answer is . . . three to four hours.

No, Really, How Long Will It Last?
NASCAR starts around February with the Daytona 500 and ends in November.

Scoring

There is some really complicated scoring system in which the winning driver gets 180 points, and the driver who comes in second place gets 170 points. The score decreases by five points for each driver in third through sixth place. For drivers in seventh through eleventh place, the score goes down by four points. You see where this is going. Drivers also get bonus points for leading a **lap** (one revolution) around the track. Only one driver gets five points for leading the most laps at the end of a race. What are these points for, car washes? No. The top twelve drivers go head to head at the end of the season, and the one with the most points wins. NASCAR nerds use all these points to keep up with the statistics on their favorite driver, to see if he's in the best twenty-five over the past six races and stuff like that.

Soccer (Formally Known as Associated Football)

Ancient civilizations played a version of soccer thousands of years ago, but England refined the game in the mid-1800s, creating the laws of the game that became the basis for the way soccer is played today. It's the most popular sport in the world, except in the United States, it seems, because football is our number one! It's pretty funny, though; every other country calls soccer "football." In Spanish, the term for American football is *futbol Americano*. However, thanks to Beck's (er, David Beckham's) multimillion-dollar contract with the Los Angeles Galaxy and the increased coverage of the World Cup, soccer may be on an upswing here. I mean, in 2007 the New York Red Bulls against FC Barcelona at Giants Stadium drew almost 80,000 people.

The atmosphere at a soccer match is totally different from that of a football game. Everyone is always on the edge of his seat, since the clock is never stopped, and there are songs and chants and beer and corn on the cob covered in cheese and guys taking their shirts off and swinging them around over their heads.

"GOOOOOOOOOOOOALLLLLLLLLL!"—As the Announcers Like to Say

So, the goal of the game is to, well, make a goal. Although, interesting enough, there are often **draws**, or ties, that represent the fairest outcome of the game. Despite its reputation as a hooligan sport, soccer has lots of rules of respect. And the players aren't crawling all over one another, which does tend to make it seem a bit more dignified. Instead, they're racing down the field, **dribbling** the ball, which isn't the same as in basketball, obviously. In soccer, you cannot touch the ball with your hands, unless you're the **goalkeeper** or performing a **throw-in** (one way to restart the action if the soccer ball crosses one of the sidelines by throwing the ball back onto the field with both hands and both feet on the ground). The defense can attempt to take back the ball by **intercepting passes** or stealing, but watch out for those **fouls**! The other team can be awarded **free kicks**—that is, they kick the ball toward the goal from the spot where the foul occurred—for these.

Player positions are simple: There are the goalkeepers; the **forwards,** who attack the opposition to try to score; **fullbacks**, who try to guard the goal to stop the opposition before it can score; and the **midfielders**, who act as liaisons between the forwards and the fullbacks.

Laws of the Game

Even though some of the terminology and player positions are similar to those in American football, soccer seems to be a much more "gentlemanly" sport. The English, known for their manners, created the laws of the game (there are seventeen laws in all), and the Fédération Internationale de Football Association (FIFA), soccer's governing body, tries to make sure that players adhere to them. For instance, there's handshaking and helping players up off the field. It's a bit different with some of the game's spectators, who can get rowdy. Sometimes there are political or sectarian tensions, and "football hooligans" are football, er, soccer club members who get out of control. Their intention is clear: They're looking for fights.

The soccer geeks I know, though, are some of the most refined sports fans I've come across. Take Miguel Banuelos, an Anglophile who dresses sharp and has a passion for rare Oasis B-sides. He has many reason for enjoying the game: "It's fast and flows well, and doesn't stop every couple seconds like American football. There are lots of understood rules of respect; it's not senselessly violent and is stylishly played. It's a global sport, and has a rich history complete with songs and stories. Also, its still a fringe sport here in the States, so all the fans are pretty die-hard and intellectual about it." So what does his girlfriend, Emilie, think? "She likes the athleticism and global nature, and doesn't mind watching games since they only last about ninety minutes. She just thanks God that I don't like football or baseball, and considers soccer the lesser of all the sporting evils."

So there you go. Soccer equals the lesser of all the sporting evils.

How Long Will It Last?

A game is ninety minutes long, and it's split into halves. The clock does *not* stop, there are *no* time-outs, but the referee may add time to the end of the game, depending on how often the game was stopped. No one knows how much time that's going to be! It's a mystery to everyone except the ref. But what's awesome about this is that the game goes *so fast*—if you leave the room for one second, you're guaranteed to miss a goal. That's how it always works for me, at least.

No, Really, How Long Will It Last?

The season differs among leagues, but basically, you can count on there being a match somewhere in the world all year long.

Scoring

A goal is one point. If the score is tied at the end of the game, it ends in a draw or a tie. If it can't end in a draw because of qualifying reasons, then it goes into overtime and the first team to score wins. If neither team scores, they can use a **penalty-kick tiebreaker** or **shootout** to figure out a winner.

Hockey

To me, hockey is a much more violent version of soccer, but on ice. An ex of mine was hockey obsessed. Since he was from New York, his team of choice was the New York Rangers, with Mark Messier and little Theo Fleury, the brawler. The Rangers became my team, as well. We'd attend games whenever we could, and they were always so aggressive—I mean, really aggressive. Physicality is encouraged in the form of **checking** (in which another player looks as if he's pushing a player away from him with his shoulder), but **elbowing**, **high-sticking**, and **crosschecking** (shoving into a player with your stick held with both hands in front of your body) aren't allowed, and those moves sometimes lead to brawls. Hockey is famous for its fights between players. The crowd encourages this, and cheers them on. It's like two sports in one! As soon as you see a player throw down his stick and whip his gloves off, you know it's on. However, the fights started getting so bad that in 2005 the National Hockey League (NHL) started laying down some major penalties, including fining a head coach whose player instigated a fight. That didn't stop the huge 2007 melee between the Buffalo Sabres and the Ottawa Senators, though—every single player on the ice got into it at once!

But listen, hockey's not all about fighting, even though it's an aggressive sport. All the players are trying to do is get that little rubber disc, the **puck**, in the net.

Modern hockey originated in Canada. In 1875, the first organized indoor game was played in Montreal. One of the first hockey matches in the United States took place between Yale University and Johns Hopkins University in 1893.

How Is It Played?

There are only six players on each side of the ice at one time: three **forwards** (a **center**, **left wing**, and **right wing**), two **defensemen**, and one **goaltender**. There are different styles of players, such as the **stay-at-home** defenseman, who is conservative and focuses mainly on defending against the opposite team rather than scoring. The game starts with a **face-off**, and the opposing center players try to get the puck before the other one does. You don't want to be **offsides**, or passing the puck in a forward direction to another player who is in a different zone. You also don't want to get penalized for **icing**, which is when the defensive team gets the puck away from the opposing team and hits it all the way down the rink toward the offense's net. Players also get in trouble if they enter the **crease**, or the area around the net that's the goaltender's domain, unless they're following the puck. You can't mess with the goaltender.

There are tons of penalties in hockey, some of which I already mentioned. Other common penalties are **boarding** (shoving a player into the border of the rink while checking), **hooking** (using the blade of a skate or the hook of a stick to mess with another player), and **slashing** (hitting another player with your stick). Although, honestly, players do these things a lot, and sometimes the refs just look the other way. It all comes back to that tradition of fighting in hockey, which, believe it or not, has its own laundry list of unspoken rules and etiquette. So see, it's *somewhat* civilized, right?

How Long Will It Last?

There are three periods of twenty minutes each, but take a guess how long games tend to last.

No, Really, How Long Will It Last?

For the NHL, preseason is September, regular season is October through April, and the postseason, or playoffs, is usually around April or whenever the Stanley Cup is.

Scoring

Each goal is worth one point.

What Have We Learned Here?

- Geeks' loving sports may seem like quite the shocker, but they do love them . . .
- . . . even if it's only for the statistics and fantasy leagues and cool computer programs.
- Pick a team! When you have something or someone to identify with, you can start enjoying the game.
- You don't need to know all the rules and terms to enjoy a sport.
- Sports, like all the other things mentioned in this book, are just another way of forming a bond with people. They don't need to get all meatheady and stuff.

CHAPTER 7

"To quote Isaac Asimov, 'I am not a speed reader. I am a speed understander.'"

Science Fiction and Fantasy Geeks

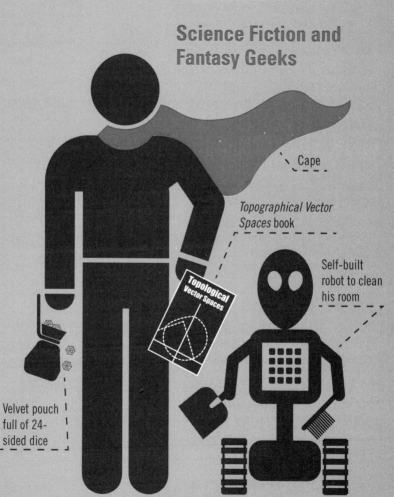

Cape

Topographical Vector Spaces book

Self-built robot to clean his room

Velvet pouch full of 24-sided dice

To sci-fi or to SF? That is the question. Like geek vs. nerd, Trekkie vs. Trekker, and Dungeon Master vs. Storyteller, the abbreviations for the science fiction genre are hotly debated. Most nerds will say that the proper abbreviation is "SF"; "sci-fi" is what non-readers of science fiction books call it, and references Hollywood bug-eyed monsters and men in silver space suits. Apparently, no one told the Sci Fi Channel or *Sci-Fi Entertainment Magazine* that. Another argument for the abbreviation "SF" is that certain nerds now claim to call the genre "speculative fiction," not "science fiction." Personally, I feel like a real elitist referring to science fiction as "SF." Plus, I used to live in California, so it makes me think of San Francisco. When someone says, "Yeah, I'm going to that SF con," I'm like, "San Francisco has its own con now?" My recommendation is, since you're a casual reader/watcher of science fiction, just call it what it is: science fiction. And if you do call it "sci-fi"? Who cares. Surely your nerd will correct you if he's offended. And let's hope he's not, 'cause that's so anal.

What's Fantasy All About?

Science fiction and fantasy are often lumped together, which is admittedly what I'm doing here, but whatever. In "The Fugitive" episode of *The Twilight Zone*, host Rod Serling delineated between science fiction and fantasy when he said, "Fantasy is the impossible made probable. Science fiction is the improbable made possible." Get it? With science fiction, it actually could happen (see *Star Trek* fans for explanation). With fantasy, ain't no way a unicorn's gonna take you down to the mall to get your elfin boyfriend a new featherlight longsword. However, there's definite crossover between science fiction and fantasy, which is why they are both included in this chapter.

Science fiction and fantasy geeks are truly birds of different feathers—or Klingons of different planets?—than your garden-variety nerds discussed in previous chapters. A lot of times, nerds interested in science fiction are interested in the *science* part of it, the rigorous detail, the possibility of abstracts becoming actualizations. Over and above anything else, they want to understand *why*—why things work, how they work, and, good god, could they make it work, too?

I'M NOT ALONE, YOU'RE NOT ALONE

Brendan Mobert, a major science fiction fan, talks about how he got that way.

▶▶ "My love for boats and astrophysics mingled into a love for all things of space travel. I became absorbed in the history of space travel: Mercury, Gemini, Apollo; Vostok, Voskhod, Soyuz, Salyute. I learned the names of the planets, their relative sizes, their relative orbits. I started to look through telescopes and very quickly found it boring: One pinpoint of light looked pretty much the same as the other. At the age of nine, I declared I would go to Mars—a dream I gave up at the age of twenty-six. Physics became the obvious prerequisite, and I listened intently to anyone willing to spend the time explaining why things worked. I can't tell you the number of times I had to read or listen to the explanation of why a rocket engine was like an escaping balloon to understand it."

And don't forget your requisite "escape from reality" reason. "A lot of sci-fi and fantasy is an escape route and often has a future full of optimism," says Ken Hahn, whose chosen career of working in special effects was influenced by *Star Wars* and *Close Encounters of the Third Kind*.

Don't See the Point Yet? Open Your Eyes!

Maybe your nerd has been trying to introduce you to his world of the space-time continuum, but you find it tiring. The characters aren't relatable; they're all cold and mechanical. There are too many numbers, too many dates, too much stuff like, "In the year 2098, there were five colonies of 700 aliens and 200 humans each, and two-thirds of those humans are actually cyborgs with more than five times the brain capacity of a normal human, who is only operating at 5 percent, so if you take away all the cyborgs, how much brain capacity do you have left?" Right. Or you think fantasy is all cloak-and-dagger, live-action-role-playing, sword-and-sorcery crap that no grownup should be into or even admit to liking, despite that sweet LARPing nerd with whom you spend every Friday night.

Well, some science fiction and fantasy *is* like that. But listen: In this chapter, I'm going to give you some examples of stuff that is actually *interesting*, has real, relatable characters, and isn't full of melodramatic, over-the-top acting or prose (except for the "so bad its good" list). Besides, odds are you grew up on some form of science fiction and fantasy. From *Dr. Who* to *Quantum Leap*, Madeleine L'Engle's *A Wrinkle in Time* to Douglas Adams' *The Hitchhiker's Guide to the Galaxy*, *The Neverending Story* to *The Lord of the Rings*, it's safe to say that you've been exposed to these genres your entire life. There's no shame in letting your inner child out. It's a relief, in fact, and a wonderful respite from what we're bombarded with on a day-to-day basis via the Internet, our jobs, our neighbors who blare music at all hours . . . I mean, there's only so much Britney Spears a girl can take.

A Brief Timeline

1726: Ahoy there! *Gulliver's Travels* by Jonathan Swift is often cited as the first example of "true" fantasy, with imaginary lands and the Lilliputians.

1818: Considered by some to be the first "official" work of science fiction, Mary Shelley's *Frankenstein* is published. It involves a mad scientist who creates a monster using body parts. I'd say it's pretty futuristic for 1818.

1835: Edgar Allan Poe's short story "The Unparalled Adventure of One Hans Pfaal" tells the story of a trip to the moon on a balloon.

1835: "Thumbelina," "The Princess and the Pea," and "The Tinder-Box" are all introduced in Hans Christian Andersen's *Fairy Tales*.

1858: Scottish author George MacDonald's *Phantastes: A Faerie Romance for Men and Women* sets the stage for works by J.R.R. Tolkien and C.S. Lewis, both of whom are heavily influenced by MacDonald.

1864: Jules Verne's *Journey to the Center of the Earth* is published. Verne writes *Twenty Thousand Leagues Under the Sea* in 1869. Both novels go on to be "re-imagined" in film and television.

1898: Aliens invade! H.G. Wells' *The War of the Worlds* starts feeding into society's paranoia.

1920s: A group of writers form a little clique and unwittingly originate the term "Lovecraft Mythos," after H.P. Lovecraft, which is later named the "Cthulhu Mythos" by writer August Derleth. The clique comprises Clark Ashton Smith, Robert E. Howard, Robert Bloch, Frank Belknap Long, Henry Kuttner, and, most notably H.P. Lovecraft, one of the most influential writers when it comes to the genres of fantasy and horror.

1932: Conan the Barbarian makes his first appearance in Robert E. Howard's *Weird Tales*.

1932: Shockingly before its time, Aldous Huxley's *Brave New World* is published.

1937: One ring to rule us all! J.R.R. Tolkien's *The Hobbit* is published.

1939: We're off to see the Wizard! The *Wizard of Oz* is released.

1940s–1950s: This is the golden age of science fiction, not to be confused with "the golden age of science fiction is twelve." (See Important Terminology, page 155)

1949–1954: C.S. Lewis's seven-book series *The Chronicles of Narnia* is published.

1949: *The Magazine of Science Fiction and Fantasy* launches. Young nerds rejoice.

1949: One of the biggest literary influences on modern science fiction, as well as popular culture in general, is published.

George Orwell's *1984* and the subsequent word "Orwellian" became synonymous with totalitarianism.

1950s: This is a great time for classic science fiction. *Them!*, *Invasion of the Body Snatchers*, *Forbidden Planet*, *The Thing*, and more films based on notorious science fiction stories are hits at the box office and pave the way for modern interpretations of science fiction.

1951: The movie poster cries, "From out of space . . . a warning and an ultimatum!" *The Day the Earth Stood Still* hits theaters.

1953: *The Quatermass Experiment* debuts on British television and is considered the first significant science fiction series.

1954–1955: The three volumes of *The Lord of the Rings* are published.

1964: Stanley Kubrick's *Dr. Strangelove Or: How I Learned to Stop Worrying and Love the Bomb* is released; Peter Sellers perfects the mad scientist role.

1965: Frank Herbert's novel *Dune* is released.

1968: *2001: A Space Odyssey* hits theaters. "Just what do you think you're doing, Dave?" becomes a famous line.

1968: Actor Charlton Heston utters some of the most awesome lines in cinematic history in *Planet of the Apes*.

1974: I cast Invisibility! From those who would judge my D&D, that is. Gary Gygax and Dave Arneson introduce Dungeons & Dragons.

1975: British science-fiction-and-fantasy-satire film *Monty Python and the Holy Grail* is considered the epitome of geek humor. *See it.*

1977: *Star Wars* and *Close Encounters of the Third Kind* are released.

1979: In space, no one can hear you scream. *Alien* is released and launches designer H.R. Giger into the spotlight.

1982: Robert E. Howard's *Conan the Barbarian* is adapted into a film.

1984: The world is introduced to the cyberpunk genre by William Gibson's *Neuromancer.*

1984: "I'll be back." Guess what I'm talking about!

1995: Brad Pitt's role as Jeffrey Goines is one of the biggest mindfucks of the film *Twelve Monkeys.*

1997: The book *Harry Potter and the Philosopher's Stone* by J.K. Rowling is released. What more can I say?

1999: Whoa. What is *The Matrix*? Well, in this case, it's the only film worth watching out of the eventual trilogy.

2001: The film adaptation of *Harry Potter and the Philosopher's Stone* is released. It grosses almost a billion dollars worldwide.

Important Classics and Terminology You Should Know

There are several—well, okay, many—building blocks of science fiction. A lot of them you may have been exposed to in school, so if you're already familiar with the Bradburys and the Asimovs, great. If not, consider this your super-short crash course.

"Classics" (Science Fiction) is just an easy way for me to cram in more recommendations that are total science fiction classics that I didn't have room to discuss. We'll look at literature, film, and television classics as well as important terminology you should definitely know:

Literature

Childhood's End by Arthur C. Clarke: Aliens invade Earth to do *good*, not evil, by ridding the world of disease, fear, and unhappiness. At least that's what the human race thinks.

Foundation by Isaac Asimov: You might know of Asimov's book *I, Robot*, which was made into a movie starring Will Smith. Well, *Foundation*'s not it, but it introduces you to the fun concept of psychohistory. Anything with the prefix "psych" is fun. And speaking of fun, just in case you thought science fiction writers were all serious without senses of humor, you should know about the "Asimov-Clarke Treaty of Park Avenue." While Asimov and Arthur C. Clarke were sharing a cab ride down Park Avenue in New York City, they decided that when asked who the best science fiction writer was, Asimov would say Clarke, and Clarke would say Asimov—thus the dedication in Clarke's book *Report on Planet Three*: "In accordance with the terms of the Clarke-Asimov treaty, the second-best science writer dedicates this book to the second-best science-fiction writer."

Fahrenheit 451 by Ray Bradbury: Bradbury's probably one of the most well-known science fiction and fantasy writers in the world. Most people I know were assigned to read *Fahrenheit 451* in their English classes, and for some of them the book sparked further interest in Bradbury and the science fiction/fantasy genre. He also wrote *Something Wicked This Way Comes*, and the 1983 film adaptation scared the crap out of me.

Stranger in a Strange Land by Robert A. Heinlein: Free love! Valentine Michael Smith is a Martian who comes to live on Earth. He decides to become a preacher, who's more like a cult leader, with a religion based on plenty of sex and an "I'm okay, you're okay" attitude. I disagree with a lot in this book—thought not necessarily Michael's religion—and I'm sure that the book is offensive to more women then men. But hey, it's a "classic."

Film

2001: A Space Odyssey: This 1968 film is based very loosely on Arthur C. Clarke's story *The Sentinel*. Don't worry: No one gets the ending.

Metropolis: Released in 1927, it's considered one of the first real sci-fi films. It's about the upper-city dwellers, who are planners and thinkers, versus the lower-city dwellers, who are worker bees. There's classism and a robot that's an exotic dancer. Oh, and it's a silent film. Watch if you dare.

The War of the Worlds: Check out the 1953 film adaptation of H.G. Wells's novel about an alien invasion. I happen to prefer the 1938 Orson Welles radio version, which supposedly initiated mass panic from the public, who actually *believed* the fake news bulletins about an alien invasion. I guess they forgot it was Halloween.

Television

V: This mid-1980s show is about "visitors" trying to take over Earth. The series was awesome for one reason: The aliens are *lizards* disguised as humans, and they want to imprison the humans so they can *eat them*!

The Outer Limits: "There is nothing wrong with your television. Do not attempt to adjust your picture." Thus started each episode of the weekly series *The Outer Limits*, which was like *The Twilight Zone* but with more science.

Lost in Space: "Danger, Will Robinson!" *Lost in Space*, a 1960s black-and-white series, had one of the best robot friends a kid could ask for.

Important Terminology you should, nay, must know.

Cyberpunk: This genre is marked by the combination of technology and gritty reality. It's also associated with industrial music. A good example is *Tetsuo: The Iron Man*, an incredibly bizarre, intense Japanese film billed as the "merging of flesh and metal." Basically, people morph into machines while still retaining some of their human features—like *The Fly* but with inorganic material. David Cronenberg's *eXistenZ* is another example. Also, tons of anime falls under the "cyberpunk" genre, such as *Akira*, *Ghost in the Shell*, *Bubblegum Crisis*, and *Appleseed*.

Dystopia: This term refers to a bleak society marked by violence and oppression, which is prevalent in science fiction.

Elvish: the language of elves, created by author J.R.R. Tolkien

Fanfic: short for "fan fiction"

Filk: This is science fiction folk music. Well, sort of. It's more like a musical community, which began with the singing of songs at science fiction and fantasy conventions. Expect to hear lyrics such as "Ho, the band of faeries, dance through the night." For some reason, there are an awful lot of filk songs about cats.

Frak: the "F word" cleaned up for network use in *Battlestar Galatica*

FTL: "faster than light" in *Battlestar Galactica*

Grok: This term comes from Heinlein's *Stranger in a Strange Land*. If you grok something, you understand the concept to a point that you *become* the concept, and you *grow* the concept. But it also can mean that you just "get it."

Hard SF: science fiction that uses science or technology as its basis, and consists of concepts that actually *could* happen with advances in that science or technology (for example, *2001: A Space Odyssey*)

Re-imagined: You'll hear this term a lot in reference to science fiction and fantasy television and film. It's a nice way of saying, "We remade the original to our liking."

Replicant: the term for androids, or well-designed robots, in the film *Blade Runner*

Robophobia: an extreme, irrational fear of robots, common in *Doctor Who*

Skiffy: a derogatory term for bad science fiction (for example, *Battlefield Earth*)

Soft SF: This term refers to science fiction that relies on a futuristic setting and takes liberties with reality and the probability of certain actions. This type of science fiction also focuses more on the "social science" aspects of a story, such as psychology. In movies like *Serenity*, there's a lot of "suspension of disbelief."

Speculative fiction: Quite a few SF fans and authors prefer this term when referencing works. Speculative fiction usually covers both science fiction and fantasy, since by nature these genres cause one to, well, think (or speculate) a lot.

"The golden age of SF is twelve": SF fans usually refer to the "golden age" as the age when they first became fans. Most often it's during adolescence, hence the reference to "twelve."

Trekkies/ers: These are big-time fans of *Star Trek*. They're fans to the point of relating every single conversation back to *Star Trek*. For example, say a Trekker's wife asks, "Hey, honey, will you walk the dog?" He might reply, "You know, in *Star Trek* TOS episode number five, 'The Enemy Within,' the transporter malfunctioned, and it was a Space Dog that helped Scotty figure out what went wrong, and . . ." Anyway, the term "Trekkies" is somewhat derogatory (because supposedly it makes *Star Trek* fans sound "crazy"); "Trekkers" is the preferred term.

Vulcans: In *Star Trek*, this is a race that lives solely on reason and logic; emotion does not compute.

Whovians: *Doctor Who* fans

Worldcon: short for the World Science Fiction Convention, where the Hugo Award, a prestigious science fiction award, is given out

The Best of the Worst
It's so very, very easy to go so very, very wrong in science fiction and fantasy. However, usually the very, very bad books, films, and TV shows are the ones that become cult classics in the "so bad it's good" genre. Here are five films to check out:

Battlefield Earth (2000): In this movie based on L. Ron Hubbard's book *Battlefield Earth*, Scientologist John Travolta stars as the leader of the alien race Psychlos. Roger Ebert put it best in the *Chicago Sun-Times*: "*Battlefield Earth* is like taking a bus trip with someone who has needed a bath for a long time. It's not merely bad; it's unpleasant in a hostile way."

Dungeons & Dragons (2000): With a surprising all-star cast (Jeremy Irons, Thora Birch, the Wayans brothers), this movie *could* have been a great fantasy film. Alas, fans of the role-playing game were astonished to see that the movie had *absolutely nothing* to do with the game. The special effects are worse than *Babylon 5*'s, and the dialogue consists of stuff such as, "This is like some magic game gone horribly wrong!" You don't say. Jeremy

Irons's "Let the blood rain from the sky!" command sounds as if he's gargling snot.

Flash Gordon (1980): What makes this update of the comic classic movie so bad that it's good? The soundtrack by Queen, the movie's total over-the-top-ness, and the 1980s lasers. It's like an even more sci-fi version of *The Rocky Horror Picture Show*.

Leprechaun 4: In Space (1996): This fourth movie in the *Leprechaun* series is so outrageous that you can't help but laugh the whole way through it. The hero travels through space to marry an alien queen so he can glom onto her title. Leprechaun gets pissed off and wants the princess as his own, so he follows our hero into space. May I repeat: Leprechaun follows our hero *into space*. The only leprechaun movie more out of control than this one is *Leprechaun: Back 2 Tha Hood*.

Star Wars Holiday Special (1978): Chewbacca's *family*? His goofy, totally annoying *son*? Han Solo pushing a stormtooper to his death out of their tree house? *DO NOT WANT*!

Getting to Know the Facts—Beginner Level

As I mentioned before, I wanted to ease you into science fiction and fantasy with some suggestions that happen to feature relatable or hot characters as well as a bit of humor and issues that are interesting to women. Now get frakin' going. Don't be intimidated by the length of most science fiction and fantasy books! If you don't like them, at the very least you can use them as stand-ins for your footstool.

Literature

The Hobbit by J.R.R. Tolkien

The Lord of the Rings may be canon when it comes to standards in the fantasy genre, but *The Hobbit* is right up there with it (along with other classics such as Madeleine L'Engle's *A Wrinkle in Time* and, more recently, *Harry Potter*). Remember Frodo Baggins, *LOTR* hero? Well, *The Hobbit* tells the story of his uncle, Bilbo, and introduces us to Gandalf (who tricks Bilbo into performing a heist of the dragon Smaug's treasure), Rivendell, the Ring, and Gollum. Tolkien creates a world so vast that it's easy to get lost in, and you'll start to think the characters are actually *real*. So I didn't take it too hard when the kids in my elementary school referred to me as a "hobbit" due to my short stature. I just thought, "Hmph, I'll show them when I get the Ring."

The Handmaid's Tale by Margaret Atwood

Margaret Atwood sucked me in with her novel *Cat's Eye*, and I've been a fan ever since. I've always been surprised and pleased that she's included in the largely boys-only club of speculative fiction; her two novels that could be considered as such, *The Handmaid's Tale* and *Oryx and Crake*, include a heavy dose of female-specific topics that definitely will appeal to you.

In the mid-twenty-first-century Republic of Gilead (formerly the United States), society is ruled by a theocratic, totalitarian government that controls all aspects of its citizens' lives. Women have been relegated to an extremely subservient position. Put it this way: All public signs now comprise pictures because women are not allowed to read. Offred, a handmaid (one of four titles now assigned to women), was an ordinary housewife with a husband and child before the theocracy arrested her. She now lives as a servant, good only for how fertile her womb is. Eventually, Offred can no longer accept her subservient position. Spurred by an illicit affair, she gains courage to contact Mayday, a female underground railroad offering sanctuary to the north.

Compared to *Brave New World* and *1984* (both high school English staples) for its dystopian society, *The Handmaid's Tale* is not a light read, to say the least. But it's very satisfying whenever I feel that our society is drowning in testosterone and fanatical leaders who govern based on religion. Eff the patriarchy, ladies.

Television

Doctor Who (originally ran from 1963 to 1989; re-imagined as a series in 2005)

Doctor Who is a British institution about a time-traveling doctor known simply as The Doctor. His method of time travel is the awesomely named TARDIS, or Time And Relative Dimensions in Space, and he is lucky enough to have access to fabulous weapons such as the glitter gun. I want a glitter gun! The Doctor runs across enemies such as alien races the Daleks and the Cybermen (note: the glitter gun kills the Cybermen!), robotic mummies, and yetis. A robotic yeti is the coolest, funniest thing ever. The original series is so mod and sci-fi. Yes, I mean "sci-fi" in every sense of the abbreviation. It's worth watching just from a fashion and design standpoint. Check out the Movellans' silver wigs and shiny white jump suits. I don't know about you, but I know what *I'm* wearing on my next date night. If you're looking for a little less kitsch, try watching the new series.

Babylon 5 (1994 to 1998)

Since I covered *Stargate SG-1* and *Stargate Atlantis* very briefly in Chapter 5, I have to recommend *Babylon 5*. I am not a fan, even though nerds and geeks canonize it. I mean, the aliens look as if they have pumpkin stems for heads . . . or hats . . . or whatever those things are supposed to be. But check out a lot of science fiction geeks' top-ten lists, and you'll find *Babylon 5* often at number one. All I can tell you is that it contains the elements that would make it number one: the space wars, often against earth, as well the alien races and planetary legislature and totalitarianism that must be rebelled against. Plus, it takes place in the 2200s, so there's a possibility that some of this stuff may *actually happen*, right?

Film

Blade Runner (1982)

Remember way back in Chapter 1 when I recommended the video game *BioShock* and said that playing it was almost like watching a movie? Well, if you want to see the real thing (relatively speaking), watch *Blade Runner*. It's the story of Rick Deckard (Harrison Ford) and his attempts to "retire" revolting replicants, humanoid robots that are almost indistinguishable from humans, save their lack of empathy. Cool, calm, and collected replicant leader Roy Batty (Rutger Hauer) is his perfect foil. The movie's set in Los Angeles in 2019, which is pretty weird when you consider that 2019 is coming up fast. Will L.A. become one dark cesspool with 700-story buildings and revolting replicants? One can only hope. Ha! Just kidding. In any case, *Blade Runner* goes well beyond science fiction films that came before it, relying heavily on noir images such as the femme fatale, the clash between past and future, and the examination of the essence of humanity. No, this isn't a light, happy-go-lucky film, but you can relate to the characters, and you will cry. At least I did. On the lighter side, take a good hard look at Pris's makeup, and tell me what over-the-hill "shock rocker" co-opted that look.

Labyrinth (1986)

Did you think my second recommendation was going to be *The Lord of the Rings*? If you're dating any type of nerd or geek, you've already seen it, and you *liked* it. Orlando Bloom's Legolas? Swoon.

So let's dig deep back into the annals of foxy leading men and fantasy history with *Labyrinth*. The last feature film to be directed by Jim Henson (creator of the Muppets) before his death, *Labyrinth* tells the story of RPGer Sarah. She becomes so involved in acting out her book *Labyrinth* that she wishes away her little brother to goblin king Jareth, played by David Bowie, who is hot, hot, hot, despite his puffy shirt. Sarah has thirteen hours to find her way out of Jareth's labyrinth, and if she fails, then baby bro gets turned into a goblin and she loses him forever. It's quite a thinly veiled warning not to let your fantasy life overshadow your real life, yes? Some of the creatures in the labyrinth befriend Sarah and help her on her quest—other creatures not so much. Since this was before computer-generated imagery, the creatures are all big puppets, so even the evil monsters look cute. I also recommend Jim Henson's *The Dark Crystal* as well as 2007's *Pan's Labyrinth*.

Getting to Know the Facts—Moving Beyond Beginner

Okay, so you're done watching the entire first season of *Doctor Who*, and your nerd wasn't psyched about the David Bowie crush. In this section, I'm going to introduce you to stuff that's a bit longer and/or more cultish. You're ready for it.

Literature

The Left Hand of Darkness by Ursula K. Le Guin

Proving that science fiction isn't just a man's genre, Ursula K. Le Guin's writing has been called "feminist science fiction" and has received numerous prestigious awards. *The Left Hand of Darkness* is a science fiction staple. Genly Ai is sent as a representative from the collective Ekuman to get the planet Gethen to join the collective. Gethen is an ultra-bizarro world that's going through its glacial period, with asexual beings who morph into males or females once a month so they can reproduce. Gethen wants nothing to do with the Ekuman, so Genly Ai sets out on this massive journey to convince them otherwise, and of course, is waylaid by all sorts of trouble. His new BFF from Gethen,

Estraven, helps him through his journey, and the book becomes just as much about their relationship as Genly Ai's quest. Le Guin is one of those science fiction authors who use alien culture as commentary on human culture, and you can bet that she thought out every single detail, down to Estraven's name.

Jonathan Strange & Mr. Norrell by Susanna Clarke

This 800-page whale of a book comes recommended by Sunny Zobel, longtime science fiction and fantasy lover. She's assured me that the length isn't something to be intimidated by; as a matter of fact, the book will suck you in so hard that you'll almost want it to be longer. So why should you undertake this task? Sunny says, "Come on, it's about magic! It's Regency England/Age of Napoleon, doddering stuffy Brits, grand ballrooms, war and muck and ancient magical texts, spiteful jinn, and jealousy, love, arrogance, ignorance, and friendship. And did I mention it's about magic? Kind of like Jane Austen (descriptive lilt and pinpoint accuracy) meets Shakespeare (the drama side) meets *Harry Potter* for grownups. Not that kids couldn't like it, but it's pretty grand and speaks more to someone who is well-read and well-seasoned by life." Isn't that you?

Television

Red Dwarf (1988 to 1999)

Let me throw a curve ball at you with this British science fiction comedy, just to prove that not everything set in the future has to be "epic" or deadly serious. Besides, who does quirky comedy better than the Brits? Did you like *Shaun of the Dead*, *The Office*,

Monty Python, *Absolutely Fabulous*, or *The Young Ones*? You'll like *Red Dwarf*. It centers around Dave Lister and Arnold Rimmer, two polar opposites stuck on a spaceship together. Lister's the happy-go-lucky type, and Rimmer's the strictly-by-the-book guy, sort of like the girl in your fifth-grade class who got super aggro when you used the "wrong" colors in art and insisted that no one's hair could be blue, *ever*. Well, just as Manic Panic showed that girl, Lister shows Rimmer that not everything is meant to be so rigid. The show has spawned tons of inside jokes and catch phrases. You'll be able to attract fellow *Red Dwarf* fanatics just by uttering the phrase, "Hey, who's the *smeghead* who left her stinky tuna fish in the fridge?"

Battlestar Galactica (2005 to present)

Based on the original 1978–1980 TV series, *Battlestar Galactica* is definitely a relatable "space opera." The Cylons (a borg-type race) and the humans have been at war for centuries, and the series picks up at the point in which the Cylons are destroying the humans' planets, called the Twelve Colonies. A small group of humans is able to flee the chaos on the ship *Galactica*. They're searching for a new planet, the thirteenth colony, Earth. *But* (and you knew there was a "but" in there), the Cylons can disguise themselves as humans, and they've infiltrated the ship. They're limited to the forms they can take and, of course, one of the forms is that of Number Six, a thin, beautiful blonde with Angelina Jolie lips. Sigh. Fanservice! Overlook that stereotypical casting, though, because the show is really good, and it does go on to feature some strong female characters.

Each episode focuses on different people on the ship, so you really get to know the refugees from the Twelve Colonies and feel a personal connection with them. You *care* about them. Every single person I know who likes *Battlestar Galactica* says, "You know, I'm totally not a science fiction fan, but this show has got me hooked." There's a lovely cinematic quality to the show, and the acting is so much better than the acting in most televised science fiction series. There are even certain episodes that will have you squirming in your seat, anxious, wondering what's going to happen next.

Film

Brazil (1985)

Continuing in the vein that science fiction doesn't have to be all serious aliens and stuff, Terry Gilliam's *Brazil* is like *1984* meets *Monty Python*—maybe because Gilliam was part of the Monty Python comedy troupe. But don't expect light comedy; *Brazil* is definitely a dark satire. Bumbling bureaucrat Sam Lowry is trying to find his dream girl while mired in a dead-end job and suffering under the weight of a totalitarian government in a, you guessed it, retro-futuristic *dystopian* society! (Sorry, there are only so many ways you can say "dark, depressing, crime-ridden, etc.," and I think I have run out of them.) Gilliam has flat-out said that his loose trilogy of films, starting with the awesome *Time Bandits* and ending with *The Adventures of Baron Munchausen*, are meant as a form of escapism from everyday life, and they offer a satirical, scathing take on society. *Brazil* is definitely a tough movie for some; it's considered "an acquired taste," which is what your geek will say about most of his stuff. However, he may disagree with this assessment, as Steve Hahnel does: "I think it's easy for most people to love. It's also easy to point to current events and therefore the prophetic nature of *Brazil*. I love it for all its technical and visionary properties, but foremost I love it for its underlying warmth, humor, and imagination. As scary as it is funny, *Brazil* is a movie I can't watch often, but it rewards equally when I do. Plus, it's the finest role Robert DeNiro was ever given." Be sure to get the "right" version of *Brazil*; try the Criterion Collection edition.

The Sword and the Sorcerer (1982)

I was thinking about recommending *Primer* here, which I guess is what I'm doing anyway since I'm talking about it. However, *Primer* is pretty obtuse. It was written, directed, and produced by mathematician and former engineer Shane Carruth, and in no way, shape, or form does Carruth attempt to explain anything in the film. Four engineers design a high-temperature superconductor, and you're just expected to know how conductivity works—which, if you're a nerd, you do. Anyway, one of the interesting and accidental facets of the superconductor is the ability to travel through time, and the film goes on to explore the ramifications of such a machine. Carruth is heavy on the philosophical conversations, so if you happened to be a philosophy major in college, this will really flip your switch. *Primer* is *cerebral*, and won the Grand Jury Prize at the 2004 Sundance Film Festival. Made by a nerd for nerds, it speaks Super Nerd language. Too much for you? You're tired and hung-over? Okay, why don't you go watch *The Sword and the Sorcerer*, which is what I was going to recommend here anyway. But if you're up for a challenge, watch *Primer*.

What Have We Learned?

- Science fiction can be abbreviated as "sci-fi" or "SF," and I honestly wish that people didn't have a preference.
- Nerds, distilled down to their essence, really want to know *how things work*.
- Science fiction and fantasy are attractive to geeks because of their focus on technology and science, plus they offer a huge dose of escapism.
- Science fiction and fantasy books and films are long and involved, but worth the investment.
- Your geek or nerd likes to ponder the outcomes of impossible situations in which he might be put to the challenge just as the hero is.
- And speaking of heroes, I really haven't mentioned them up until this point, but try to make your geek feel as if he's your hero every once in a while. Say something along the lines of "Oh, I don't know, Hercules doesn't really do it for me, you know? I much prefer men who are built like you."

"No one will really be free until nerd persecution ends."
—Gilbert,
Revenge of the Nerds

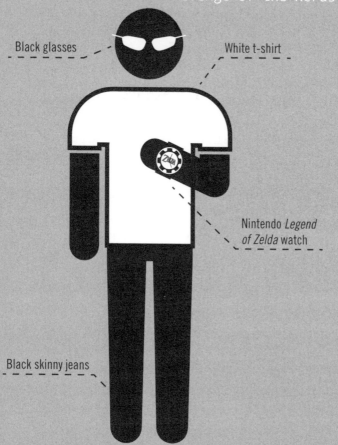

Black glasses

White t-shirt

Nintendo *Legend of Zelda* watch

Black skinny jeans

Wait, what? We're done? But . . . but . . . what about computers and programming? Biochemistry? Physics? Math? You know, the actual building blocks of nerd-dom?

Well, here's the thing: Those interests—or, rather, fields of study—aren't so nerdy anymore. The people who study them, on the other hand, probably are, but it's a sure bet that their interests fall into one of the categories I've examined in this book. The guys who work or study in these fields may lack social skills, but doesn't everyone who is dedicated to his or her craft?

Will the Entire Human Race Evolve Into Nerds One Day?

Another reason why these fields aren't considered quite so nerdy now is because, well, people need them. We need the computer programmers not only to create new pieces of software so we can make our "Cutest Dog in the World" iBooks and take apart our machines when something goes wrong with them, but also to make sure that the computers inside our cars are running without any bugs and our financial information is protected online. We need the biochemists to become pharmacologists so they can make sure the thousands of drugs on the market don't happen to, you know, give someone a heart attack because they interact with asparagus or something. Get the picture? And the more these people are needed, the higher their salaries are, which leads to more incentive for others to work in the same fields, therefore more of these people exist in the world, making them more a norm than an anomaly.

Random Computer Geek Terms You Should Know

Still baffled by your computer nerd? Well, I'll drop some brief knowledge, and then you can let your IT geek do the rest. Honestly, I've never met an IT geek who didn't take pride in his skills. Even if the directive is as simple as "reboot," he looks manly flipping a switch on a woman's computer and saying, "Okay, done," as if it were magic or something. April, who works in sales at a clothing company, even faked computer problems so that she could talk to her company's IT guy, on whom she had a crush. "He was so badass," she sighs. "Although, by the time my hard drive crashed for real, he was still telling me to 'reboot' because he was on to me."

Applications: These are programs or groups of programs that you use on your computer to do things, such as word processing, creating spreadsheets, and making dreaded PowerPoint presentations

Byte: It's a unit of storage on your computer. Geeks like gigabytes and terabytes.

Cache: This is the place in your Web browser that keeps track of the Web pages you have visited. IT guys like to tell you to "empty your cache" when something's wrong with your Internet connection.

DOS: Short for "Disk Operating System," it was a way of communicating with one's computer waaay back in the 1980s and early 1990s that consisted of typing commands in order to do something. Tech nerds used DOS up until 2000.

IP address: This is your computer's identifying number when it's on the Internet. Now you know what your geek's *There's No Place Like 126.40.0.0* t-shirt means.

Linux: A free operating system developed mainly by Linus Torvalds, Linux is not a proprietary system, which means that no company owns it. Geeks love it. But if they ask you, "Do you know Linux?" do not be afraid to say no. They would love to teach you.

Meta: Internet geeks like to say this a lot. Technically, it means "all encompassing."

Network: This is a connected group of computers, such as your work network. To nerds, "network" does not mean drinking all the free booze at an industry party in order to relate to coworkers more easily. Nor does it mean hooking up with the IT guy in the server room (see "server room" below).

Operating system: It's what your computer uses to run programs, such as Windows on PCs or Leopard on Macs.

Platform: Similar to an operating system, a platform is what your computer runs on. No, I don't mean electricity or batteries. Think Mac OS X or Windows.

Plug-in: This is an application added to your Internet browser to allow it to do certain things such as play video.

RAM: Short for "random access memory," it's a type of computer data storage.

Reboot: This is the standard IT guy answer to any computer problem. "Doug, my Windows won't open." "Reboot." "Doug, my computer is saying 'fatal error.'" "Reboot." "Doug, my computer seems to be smoking like it's on fire." "Reboot." It means the same thing as "restart."

Server/host computer: This is a computer running software that provides documents to the World Wide Web. Your IT guy may use a "server problem" as an excuse to take breaks during the workday. You: "Doug, why haven't I gotten any e-mail in the past seven hours?" Doug: "The server's down; working on it."

Server room: This is the place that contains the host computer—aka the place where Doug goes to hide out after too many reboots.

My Parting Words of Wisdom

1. There is no need to be intimidated by your nerd's or geek's interests. Once you start getting involved, and obtain the foundation, you're sure to realize how fun they are and want to learn more.

2. Geeks are both made and born. Thank genetics, encouraging parents, and a predisposition for asking questions and trying to figure out the world around them, even if the world around them does end up consisting of a server room.

3. Be yourself. Oh, God, did I actually say that? Ugh. I did. I couldn't think of a better way to put it. It's probably safe to say that you already have exposed your true self to your geek or nerd, but don't front on what you don't know.

4. On that note, geeks and nerds love to teach and share their often obscure knowledge. So don't be afraid to ask your geek if you don't understand something!

5. The name of the game is compromise. If you find you're still having problems with your geek's or nerd's playing *God of War* six hours a day, and you feel that it's taking away from your relationship, try to strike a compromise so he doesn't feel that you're limiting him. Say, "Hey, let's watch *Babylon 5* tonight, 'cause tomorrow night *Top Chef* is on."

6. Fandom is an international language. It bonds your nerd or geek to others and allows him to feel comfortable. Let your boy be.

7. There are different levels of nerd- and geek-dom. Where does your guy fall?

   a. **The undercover geek:** Thanks to his fashion sense and social skills, you'd never guess that he's hiding his *World of Warcraft* addiction and encyclopedic knowledge of all human-cyborg relationships.

   b. **The functioning nerd or geek**: He sort of wears his awkwardness on his sleeve, but still goes out into society and acts like a normal human being and doesn't let his obsessions rule his life.

   c. **The totally non-functioning nerd or geek:** Usually, these guys are insanely intelligent, painfully shy and introverted, and always studying *something* that they can't help inserting into casual conversation. This guy won't even know you actually like him; you'll have to sneak up on him and smack him on the head with his external hard drive or something.

8. There's a nerd and geek hierarchy. At the bottom levels, you've got your video game players, your comic and manga readers, anime collectors, toy obsessives, and science fiction and fantasy lovers. But from there, it starts

morphing into deeper nerd-dom, with *World of Warcraft*, for example. There also are online RPGers, Renaissance Faire and Society for Creative Anachronism attendees, con devotees who visit the autograph tables, geeks who display their toy collections in their living rooms, and cosplayers.

Next, there are those who enjoy LARPing (live-action role-playing, which is similar to cosplay only more serious, and usually involves fantasy or something medieval); Renaissance Faire attendees who actually travel the country with their fair as merchants, minstrels, and performers; Trekkers; people whose marriages break up because they've been virtually cheating in *Second Life*; and fanfic authors. But the pinnacle of nerd-dom, a pinnacle that almost doesn't even count as nerd-dom anymore because even the hard-core nerds eschew these guys, are the furries. Sorry, guys. You may look cute and cuddly, but everyone knows what you're up to.

9. Geeks and nerds like commitment. They like dependability.
10. At the end of the day, geeks and nerds are no different from anyone else. Wait, that's a total lie! They are different, and that's what makes them great. They have smarts, wit, and superior abilities all rolled up into one package. Who cares if they're socially awkward? Just get yours out in public and start showing him off. He's still wearing that same un-ironic computer-software-company shirt? Grab something from his closet and say, "Hey, this looks hot on you!" As a wise woman once said, "Once you go geek, you never go back."

INDEX